GRIT & JOY

HELP FOR BEWILDERED FAMILIES OF TEENS

BY
DAVE RAHN AND
EBONIE DAVIS

D6 FAMILY MINISTRY
114 BUSH RD · NASHVILLE, TN 37217 · 800.877.7030 · D6FAMILY.COM

Grit & Joy: Help for Bewildered Families of Teens

© 2025 by Dave Rahn & Ebonie Davis

Published by D6 Family Ministry

ISBN: 9781614841913

TABLE OF CONTENTS

INTRODUCTION

We believe teens can gain durable joy. Further, we think adolescents are well-suited to be our *canaries in the coal mines.* If they're in good shape, so are we. And if they're gasping for air amid toxic life fumes adults spew into circulation, we're all in trouble.

Young people will not gain vitality with Jesus through a six-month curriculum, a weekend workshop, or slick programs supported by glorious graphics and technological wizardry. It is only doable if we adults who love young people are willing to disrupt how we spend our time.

When we heard Matt Croasmun use a diving analogy, we decided to use it as the organizational framework for this book.

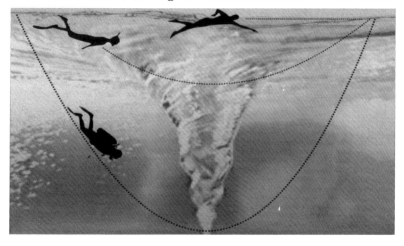

Too much of our time is spent in unreflective *surface* splash-abouts, where we "do what we do because that's what we do."[1]

We begin our book by addressing what's obvious to parents and youth ministers alike: that our young people are aimlessly splashing in surface-level activity. They're not alone in their *bewilderment.* Kids flail among others who are lost—they don't know the love of God. We adults, especially parents, need an authentic and attractive faith to help adolescents thrive.

Everyone seems to be settling for something less than what our Creator intended. Chapters 2 and 3 help us marvel about how the LORD wired us for a lovingly disruptive relationship with Him. This compels us to pierce the surface of aimless living, but too many of our well-intended efforts simply coax teens to become more thoughtful. We gain access to useful strategies that we assume can grow life effectiveness. Snorkel-level depths can expose us to underwater beauty that surface splashers can't see. But if family and ministry life dwells in these *shallows*, the priority of usefulness will disfigure our relationships. Collective restlessness, as we write about in Chapter 4, reveals how unaligned we are with love's power.

Our Lord Jesus brings surgical skill to the disruption we all need. He is especially adept at showing us the folly of hurry and helping us leverage our limited capacity for relationship to enjoy companionship with Him. We are custom fit for resilient joy, but we also share a common design. Chapter 5 explores why we need to adjust rather than to ignore our relational-life operating system.

The social science concept of *grit*[2] awakened us to the richness of understanding how biblical faith gains us a relationship with Creator God that is, as William A. Barry calls it, "a friendship like no other."[3] Exploiting Croasmun's underwater metaphor gives us the chance to explore how the good life of joy with Jesus requires deep diving. Only there can we retrieve what's most crucial to our very essence. As the psalmist expresses it, when life drives us downward—inward—we can know God's unfailing love.[4] We secure our identity with Jesus when we meet Him in the *depths* of our being and resurface with new perspective to do differently what we once did thoughtlessly. Grit sanctions our hunt for habits to disrupt aimlessness and restlessness, so we enjoy how Jesus has rigged together all the people, places, things, and moments for ultimate good. Well-aimed grit—as we describe in Chapters 6, 7, and 8—is *necessarily important* for a life built around the Great Commandment. Why? Because it's not natural for us to love God with all we've got and to love our neighbors as ourselves. A deep-diving companionship with Jesus unlocks love's disruptive power for any relationship.

This book explores how to disrupt the pace of life we've commonly adopted in order to gain the life for which we were created. We're latching on to social science research, brain science discoveries, personal experiences, practical theology, and biblical truth to offer solutions that align us with God through grit-as-faith that results in love-as-joy. Jesus masterfully altered the rhythm of those around Him; we want Him to tutor us in this process. Our kids are victims of the shallow lives we offer them; we want to disrupt their pace by changing our own. God's fourth commandment was an identity-defining pace disruptor for an entire nation. Its inclusion among the Ten gives it moral authority, and it has been incredibly fruitful for us to reflect on how this keystone habit—revisited in light of Jesus' work—can anchor our pace-disruption efforts. This book is written for those who've wondered whether life-pace change-ups are tactically crucial, *not* optional, for an authentic faith, teen-tested and fit for family

3

consumption. Our final four chapters—sandwiched by slices of grace—offers practical help through habit commendations.

Durable joy with Jesus is a legacy endowment to give the next generation. But an inheritance must be owned before it is bequeathed. This book evolved into its current form after its birth as a social science study, sponsored by the John Templeton Foundation and administrated by the Yale Center for Faith and Culture. For more than a year, we strained to do research for our inquiry. We ultimately suspended these attempts in favor of a way of understanding best gained by sharing a faith adventure together. That's when and how we experienced breakthroughs, both profound and personal. Now we simply offer this book to testify about what we are finding. Our quest has changed *us*, first of all and most of all.

A word about the "we." Writing together is a tricky, multi-layered effort, but our chief goal is to make this book as readable as we can. Much of the time the "we" means Ebonie and I stand together in what we've written. But you may have already noticed how I (Dave) am taking the lead voice in the book. Since narratives, especially, are most easily told from a personal perspective, we set up the book by using a different font so when Eb shares a story or insight from her own journey, you can easily discern who's writing what. What we both want you to know— and this is crucially important to us—is that this book is the result of a collaborative journey that has enriched us far more than we ever anticipated. Ebonie's vulnerability demonstrated courage beyond any act I could have imagined, and it represents the profound fruit of our journey together. God is good, and He gets all the glory in this story.

Adding a couple of discussion questions at each chapter's conclusion reflects our heart to help adults model a deep, more authentic faith for the adolescents they love. We hope they can *disrupt the pace* of your time together and trust Jesus will make this journey worth your while. May the teens you love bless you for showing them how to gain joy with Jesus that carries them through a lifetime.

CHAPTER 1

AIMLESS ON THE SURFACE

Why is adolescent joy so easily shattered?
hy is youth ministry not known for growing sustainable joy in young people?

Why are parents so bewildered about how to endow their teens with resilient joy?

Squeezed between houses in a west side Indianapolis neighborhood is an empty lot that Danny Marquez and friends turned into the "Purpose Park." The really cool vibe emanating from this small acreage oozes from the hull of a '64 Bonneville buried nose-down near the front of the lot. On a warm mid-July evening, young people and adults gathered in this sweet location for a "Joy & Pizza" conversation. One of the adults created a stir among the teens sitting on tree stumps when he said, "Joy is a choice." Ebonie and I perked up. *This* debate had surfaced in other locations around the country and, frankly, it was really fun to watch.

Where we land on this question is consequential. If joy is a choice, then we need intentionality to pursue this good life. Why would we ever pick a pathway that can't bring us to joy? And if large hunks of teens' time—and ours—are spent aimlessly bobbing around life's surface waters, we may need to disrupt whatever we're doing so we can pursue joy. Our sporadic joy testifies that we're not getting enough quality life return on our time investments.

Try a quick thought experiment. Recall an inconsequential experience in the last 72 hours that brought you a sudden rush of joy. For example, maybe you noticed a joy spike when you were stuck in a long line of left-turning vehicles, but you squeezed through the intersection before the light changed. Or perhaps your normally high-maintenance dog was so unusually relaxed when you needed a break that a gratitude-joy mix arose in your spirit. Push yourself to reflectively search for minutiae in your memory files. Forage among unexpected surprises. Chances are pretty good that little moments of joy flash in and out of most normal days, flying under the radar of your conscious perceptions. They're usually triggered by some event or circumstance that happens *to* us, *around* us, and *for* us. These fill our experience buckets wearing the same label: *state of joy.*

If joy is *only* a temporary state, we don't want to miss it when it drops by. It's like we're vulnerable beach toddlers, hoping life's next ocean wave is more of a pleasant splash than a knock-down crash. Intermittent pleasant surprises wash over us, but we are passive beneficiaries, not agents of control. We cannot choose what kind of waves will arrive on our shore, but if we don't make *any* choices that result in joy, isn't life one constant bob-about on the circumstantial surface of what happens to us? Too many teens and their chaotic families live in this aimless vulnerability, doing what we do without much thought about why we do it.

Pinning down a definition that can explain the range of experiences we associate with joy isn't easy. This difficulty has curbed the enthusiasm of joy-scholars looking for clarity and understanding. But positive psychologists have tackled research and concluded our experiences of joy can be explained as either a *state* or a *trait*.[5] Consider the euphoria of countless Cubs fans when, after 108 years, their team finally won a baseball World Series in 2016. Most *joy-as-state* experiences are far less dramatic, but they give birth to a similar celebratory feeling. It doesn't take a research degree to declare when occasions bring joy to victors and those who cheer them on. These are states of joy, riding the circumstantial coattails of countless big and small events every day, all over the world.

We've long understood how important friendships are to teenagers' joy. As they navigate who they are and where they're headed, they are especially vulnerable to social influences.[6] Those skimming across the surface of aimlessness are not without friends to splash around with—such hanging out needs little organizational effort. While youth ministers hope to be counted among those who make a difference in the lives of young people, parents intuitively know that no one is more responsible for rescuing their kids from aimlessness than they are.

Unfortunately, many adults share a credibility problem. We grind our way through each day and our slogging is not lost on young people. When parents come home from work a bit more diminished, teens notice the leakage. The pep in our step is barely enough for us to tackle other obligations. Work is to be life's side gig. But they—the kids we love—start to wonder if *they* fall into the category of "obligations." Quietly, desperately, a deep resolve resistant to adult influence is born in their hearts: "Not for me."

Kids are far too broken today. Unfortunately, some of this is due to how we engage them. A whopping 32% of kids point to their parents' technology use as one thing that makes them feel unimportant.[7] A recent study indicates that average users touch their phones about 2,617 times per day. The heavy users, like most of our students (who take their cues from us), touch their phones about 5,000 times per day.[8] Downstream of this "cauldron of stimulus" is an alarming spike in adolescent depression and anxiety.[9]

Psychologists coined the term "technoference" to describe the disruption that technology causes to our relationships. As Erika Christakis noted in *The Atlantic,* adults have imagined they can juggle near limitless relationship and life-management obligations because of this digital deception. They can't. And parents, especially, will poorly serve their children until they learn to trade *doing all things* for *doing less.*[10]

A conviction about the life we do *not* want is *not yet* a clear pathway for how to get the life we *do* want. Princeton professor Kenda Creasy Dean's analysis of the data from the National Study of Youth and Religion led her to a haunting conclusion: if young people have a flimsy, inarticulate faith they learned it from adults.[11] We're modeling for teens a way to live that is exhausting, unappealing, and poorly representative of the rich life God intends us to enjoy with Him. Adolescents are surface-bobbing in an ocean of aimlessness and our ministry efforts—originating from both home and church—have too often failed to be of help to them.

For everyone's sake, we think it is time to disrupt the pace—less hurry to become more deliberate; more deliberate to love better. Loving relationships need to expand, not shrink; this is especially true regarding how we connect with God. Only when we cooperate with our Creator's relational joy hard-wiring can we be ushered into the best versions of ourselves. When teens experience abandonment, we dare not dismiss it as a growth phase they will move beyond. That sort of passivity practically guarantees kids' flimsy faith. Ebonie describes such a young person, one sadly familiar to youth ministers:

Jason showed up at youth group for the first time with his older brother on a cold Wednesday evening. Why the two brothers came to our church we didn't really know. They knew some of our church teens from school, and we'd been trying to reach out to the neighboring trailer park community where they lived. Whatever their initial reason, we knew what kept them coming: dinner.

We did our best to connect with Jason, but it soon became clear that any relationship with adult youth leaders was going to be on his terms. His background was rough; his father was incarcerated. Day or night, he roamed the neighborhood, operating on his own at the tender age of 14. He'd obviously been wounded by life. Love was absent. Jason embodied the adage, "Hurting people hurt people." We learned the hard way how much havoc he could wreak in the church, like when he amused himself by convincing one third grader to punch another in the face during our neighborhood VBS outreach.

Each time he veered off track I'd say, "I love you, and God loves you, but this is not a good day for you. You need to leave today, but you can come back next week." Undeterred, he always returned. Jason persistently attended during his two-year tour of 8th grade and continued into high school.

We sought to tangibly express God's love by meeting some of his needs. He was the reason we created a tutoring program. We took groceries to his home, and gave him schools supplies. I invested in him personally, and the whole team prayed relentlessly for him. Jason, ever guarded, calmed down a bit. But we never had indications that we, or the gospel we shared, made inroads to his heart. Still, he kept coming regularly, even after his brother stopped showing up.

Occasionally, Jason seemed to forget the wall he had so carefully built. We were privileged to peek in on this teen's unfiltered joy. Even after dropping out of 9th grade and hanging around a drug house, he dropped by, albeit infrequently. Near his eighteenth birthday, he swung by the church to say goodbye. A burden to his single mom, Jason was told to move out. He would probably land far away.

Resistant to consider God's love beyond attending weekly youth group, even this small exposure kept tugging on him. He had splashed around with Jesus just enough to taste and see His unconditional love. But his life story hampered him from all but skimming across life's surface. Largely aimless, Jason's fleeting encounters with the love of Jesus never made enough sense for him to consider deeper possibilities.

Our Creator God formed us with His always loving purposes in mind, but Jason is among the millions who, for countless reasons, are lost in aimless living. And if the seemingly entrenched young person also sat down to family meals with us for years, our bewilderment hosts indescribable grief.

Before writing *A Grief Observed*, C. S. Lewis wrote an autobiography about his plunge into life with Christ, entitled, *Surprised by Joy*. His curiosity about how and when joy took place throughout his life led him into a rigorous intellectual quest for answers. Eventually, breakthrough discoveries exposed the emptiness of other worldview options, ultimately leading him to a faith in God sturdy enough to engage life's tensions with brutal honesty. Insightfully, Lewis observed that a thought *about* something is necessarily different from the object itself. More specifically, he realized that joy leaves evidence that signaled so much more—alluring clues about a deeper reality. Joy revealed a union he sought with unparalleled yearning.[12]

Lewis profoundly concluded that these frequent and familiar "stabs" of joy were not as important as he once thought except for their pointing to something beyond the experiences.[13] In dissecting his search, he discovered Christ to be not only his source of joy, but also the source of his *desire* for joy. Magnetically disruptive, Jesus pulls our attention to Him. Only then can we know the joy of His love and experience the most important life-orienting relationship of all.

Aimlessness was another characteristic of those the Bible declared to be lost, those whom Jesus explicitly targeted "to seek and to save."[14] The religious elite of his day were haughty and critical; Jesus was moved by compassion for those misled by blind guides who delighted in pouncing on lawbreakers. Jesus countered their judgmentalism with disruptive, upending love. John's record of one such beautiful showdown features Jesus asking an inescapably leveling question of legendary status:

> Jesus returned to the Mount of Olives, but early the next morning he was back again at the Temple. A crowd soon gathered, and he sat down and taught them. As he was speaking, the teachers of religious law and the Pharisees brought a woman who had been caught in the act of adultery. They put her in front of the crowd.
>
> "Teacher," they said to Jesus, "this woman was caught in the act of adultery. The law of Moses says to stone her. What do you say?"
>
> They were trying to trap him into saying something they could use against him, but Jesus stooped down and wrote in the dust with his finger. They kept demanding an

answer, so he stood up again and said, "All right, but let the one who has never sinned throw the first stone!" Then he stooped down again and wrote in the dust.

When the accusers heard this, they slipped away one by one, beginning with the oldest, until only Jesus was left in the middle of the crowd with the woman. Then Jesus stood up again and said to the woman, "Where are your accusers? Didn't even one of them condemn you?"

"No, Lord," she said. And Jesus said, "Neither do I. Go and sin no more."[15]

It's not uncommon to see aimless people—young and old alike—engage in regrettable activity. Our natural-born instincts simply can't serve us well.[16] In stark contrast to the disengaged, law-obsessed posture of the Pharisees, Jesus co-mingled love for the lost with truth for all. It *is* possible to walk among the aimless lost without becoming like them. Jesus "love-bombed" those hunkered down in self-righteousness with stories intended to disrupt their misplaced zeal. Their snooty lovelessness was at odds with God's purpose. That seemed to be the aim of a familiar parable:

Tax collectors and other notorious sinners often came to listen to Jesus teach. This made the Pharisees and teachers of religious law complain that he was associating with such sinful people—even eating with them! ...

To illustrate the point further, Jesus told them this story: "A man had two sons. The younger son told his father, 'I want my share of your estate now before you die.' So his father agreed to divide his wealth between his sons.

"A few days later this younger son packed all his belongings and moved to a distant land, and there he wasted all his money in wild living. About the time his money ran out, a great famine swept over the land, and he began to starve. He persuaded a local farmer to hire him, and the man sent him into his fields to feed the pigs. The young man became so hungry that even the pods he was feeding the pigs looked good to him. But no one gave him anything.

"When he finally came to his senses, he said to himself, 'At home even the hired servants have food enough to spare, and here I am dying of hunger! I will go home to my father and say, "Father, I have sinned against both heaven and you, and I am no longer worthy of being called your son. Please take me on as a hired servant."'

"So he returned home to his father. And while he was still a long way off, his father saw him coming. Filled with love and compassion, he ran to his son, embraced him, and kissed him. His son said to him, 'Father, I have sinned against both heaven and you, and I am no longer worthy of being called your son.'

"But his father said to the servants, 'Quick! Bring the finest robe in the house and put it on him. Get a ring for his finger and sandals for his feet. And kill the calf we have been fattening. We must celebrate with a feast, for this son of mine was dead and has now returned to life. He was lost, but now he is found.' So the party began.

"Meanwhile, the older son was in the fields working. When he returned home, he heard music and dancing in the house, and he asked one of the servants what was going on. 'Your brother is back,' he was told, 'and your father has killed the fattened calf. We are celebrating because of his safe return.'

"The older brother was angry and wouldn't go in. His father came out and begged him, but he replied, 'All these years I've slaved for you and never once refused to do a single thing you told me to. And in all that time you never gave me even one young goat for a feast with my friends. Yet when this son of yours comes back after squandering your money on prostitutes, you celebrate by killing the fattened calf!'

"His father said to him, 'Look, dear son, you have always stayed by me, and everything I have is yours. We had to celebrate this happy day. For your brother was dead and has come back to life! He was lost, but now he is found!'"[17]

God's love targets everyone. But in the passage quoted above, we see how the complaining religious leaders who disavowed such associations needed to hear something different from those aimlessly lost "notorious sinners" who came to hear Jesus teach. Those who identify most with the older brother also need love's disruption.

For now, let's embrace this reality: **adult aimlessness has put teens in double jeopardy.** They feel unloved and abandoned by people they need and are incapable of self-rescue. Too many religious elites of Jesus' day were burdensome, blind guides, not empathetic rescuers. Corrupting God's intention for the Law, they equated love with duty. Unintentionally, our youth ministries often communicate the same thing. Unwittingly, our family patterns embrace ways of life at odds with God's kingdom. Our misguided practices need Jesus' correction, so we might love God with every fiber of our beings and love others without hesitation. The Westminster Shorter Catechism's famously answers its first question by asserting our chief purpose is to glorify and enjoy God forever.[18] When we welcome the risen Christ as our indwelling, intimate Lord, He regularly disrupts our pace, takes control, bestows grace, and unleashes joy.

This is vastly different from where most young people live. They skim across the top of each day's water aimlessly, accepting fragile stabs of joy as a random life reality. Unaware or unconvinced about the possibility of abundantly joyful living with Jesus, they grow numb to any notion of life below the surface. Youth ministries and parents share the same challenge: to meet young people in this splash zone, not to entertain, appease, or momentarily ease them, but to lead them into the good life of disruptive joy with Jesus.

Joyful Disruptions

Q1. How would you describe an aimless person?

Q2. How do you make your teens feel noticed and valued?

Q3. What could you "do less" of to be more available to your teens?

CHAPTER 2

LORD OF DISRUPTIVE LOVE

Dorothy Bass observed that too often our days get swallowed up in smallness.[19] Many of us can relate to that, even though we're well aware of thick biblical truths that point to something far richer than we commonly experience:

> **GOD IS LOVE.**[20] John used the word "love" almost as many times as did the trio of other gospel writers combined. He also used "true" or "truth" over six times more often than what's recorded in the combination of the synoptics.[21] Having listened carefully to Jesus for three years, John recorded the most significant truth of all, unmatched in importance for life and ministry.
>
> **JESUS IS LORD.** This confession is most likely the earliest identifying statement among Christians, a shorthand reference to the belief that all things were created by, are sustained by, and will be worked together for the good glory of Jesus Christ.[22] The apostle Paul was tasked to make known the mysterious connectivity of all things under the Lordship of Christ.[23]
>
> **IT'S ALL GOOD.** Or it *was.* And it *will be* ultimately re-shaped for unimaginable glory. Our infinite God spoke life

into existence and declared it was all "very good." But sin is far too familiar, and it routinely disrupts any good intention we summon for daily living. If not for Jesus Christ, we'd be utterly lost. Now—in the amazement of grace beyond wonder—we can partner with Christ for good.[24]

Smack-dab in the middle of God's promises that we *can* thrive, too much evidence suggests we don't. We're clawing for hope, fighting to hang on. Days "lost to smallness" seems an accurate description for families swamped in busy activity. Because Ebonie and I have invested more than 70 combined years in some form of youth ministry, we are especially concerned about the well-being of adolescents. As we earlier suggested, they are like "canaries in the coal mine." While these birds were expendable in order to alert miners about the unseen, poisonous gasses escaping due to their digging, our beloved teens—not expendable—are gasping for air as we diminish ourselves with other pursuits. We're reminded that aimlessness is not necessarily carefree neglect. At the inarticulate core of any lost person is a gnawing ulcer of angst, quietly but persistently testifying that all is *not yet* good.

Meanwhile, the Bible tells us we can "rejoice always" and "count it all joy."[25] **It's all good?**

Too many of us are constantly busy without being paid off in joy, felt or sustained. We endure deeply dissatisfying lives. Teens are especially vulnerable. Between 2010 and 2020, those ages 18–25 reported an 139% increase in anxiety, a percentage that somewhat declines among older age groups when it stabilizes among those fifty years old and older.[26] Most experience joy as short-term surprise stabs with the duration of a Red Bull energy spike, at best.

Ask young people to describe how they experience joy, and they respond with halting uncertainty. Their default is to describe memorable moments, even surprises. Three high school girls had just won their first lacrosse game of the year in Waldorf, Maryland; their first response to our question was to describe joy by referencing this recent rarity at the last game of the season. A nurse in her mid-twenties who was in the same focus group as our lacrosse winners filibustered the entire session during another one of our "Joy & Pizza" conversations, insistently asking a counter-question as we probed about what joy meant: "Who's to say?" As frustrating as this was for those gathered who were actually *trying to agree* about some universal properties of joy, it reveals how aimlessness can become an entrenched lost state. We all make sense of the world by drawing upon how we interpret treasured personal experiences.

It can also reveal a daunting challenge to this chapter's opening trio of theological assertions. We're not unfamiliar with young people asking, "Who's to say?" It's commonly an expression of defiance rather than an honest search for someone certified with final authority. Confessing that "Jesus is Lord" is a tacit acknowledgment that *He* gets the last word. That might be why Ebonie and I cringed a bit to hear that response between pizza bites. It usually reveals the heart of someone unwilling to change their thoughts or actions.

Our young people may be especially vulnerable to experiencing only these *states* of joy. *God is Love*, but most seem untouched by this profound truth. We were formed for relationships by a Trinitarian God who has always existed in loving, mutual interdependence. Jesus came to usher us into this dance of joy. This is God's foremost plan for our formation—that we might love Him and enjoy being loved by Him. This inbred need is so crucial to our well-being that St. Augustine wrote, "Our heart is restless until it rests in You."[27] Maybe these words make teens wonder. Maybe they will chew on them. But too often, their lived reality dismisses the possibility of such joyful faith. Uneven waves of social joy come from undependable friends. Too many flail in the shallows, searching for relational footing. This is especially true among families that have exploded into fractured pieces, a too common experience among young people. The waves that pound away on their identity shores are erosive social forces, and their joy is fragile.

Adult self-neglect contributes to the storyline of adolescent aimlessness. But there's a monstrous elephant to reckon with before we pivot to explore this painful reality. If we're to gain and pass along joy with Jesus that works so "It's all good" for families and their teens, we dare not glibly sidestep life's upending adversities. Indeed, we would have to disavow the possibility of resilient, constant joy as soon as we face a tragic life-wave that comes from any place other than the vast ocean of God's love.

Ebonie's story represents the insistent power of adversity. Not until writing this book did I learn of her horrific trauma. Now I understand why her authentic joy with Jesus has made her such a valuable companion in my journey into the mysterious deep. Here's how it began.

I missed the school bus. That's how it all started. That day in 1989 I was 13, in a year of transition. My sweet grandmother who had lived with our family since I was a baby had recently moved to an assisted living facility. Because we had two working parents who left early in the morning, she had made sure we got on the bus and dinner was ready when we got home. But now we were on our own, and our home's turmoil and tension seemed to grow in her absence.

I was in my second year at a magnet middle school for performing arts, where I majored in theater, on track to go on to a performing arts high school—or maybe even more (I had, after all, landed a role on a local TV show!) But the school was not in my neighborhood, and when I missed the bus, I frustrated my parents a lot. By the time I was leaving for school, they were long gone into the city to work. On this morning, I couldn't bring myself to call and confess that I'd missed the bus—again. I decided to take the public bus, which picked up a few blocks from my house, then walk the two miles or so from the nearest bus stop to the school. The risk was that I wouldn't make it before absentee calls were made to parents, but I had to try.

My stomach was nervous the entire ride, and when I got off the bus at a familiar intersection, I realized how far a two mile walk truly was. After about five minutes of quick walking a pickup truck pulled alongside me. Inside were two men and they offered me a ride. I hesitated, remembering briefly warnings about strangers. But I still hoped I could make it to school before anyone noticed.

So, I got in the truck. I got in willingly—a fact I kept hidden for many years, even from those closest to me.

The big, stocky man got out and told me to slide in and over to the middle. We made small talk as we drove up the road toward the school. I told them my name. As we passed the school building, I pointed out to them that they had missed the turn. They exchanged glances, but the thin man continued to drive. I said, "Please stop," voice trembling, but they were silent. I knew I was in trouble.

Hours later I emerged from the apartment complex where my virginity had just been ripped from me, clutching my belongings and running for my life. I escaped through a narrow window of opportunity when the two men took a break to get high on PCP. I ran until I could run no longer, then slowed to catch my breath.

The adrenaline I used to escape gave way to trauma, and I began to sob. Moments later a small four-door sedan stopped and a brown skinned woman with a kind face asked if I needed help. She told me to get in, and for the second time that day, I did. She surveyed my disheveled appearance from her rearview mirror and asked me if I was ok. My body throbbed. The sight of the bloody sheets I'd left behind flashed through my mind. And then I remembered. I had missed the bus. Shame dropped over me like a heavy cloud for the bad decisions that put me in this position. I never answered the lady. I directed her to drop me off near my home and thanked her.

The house was noisy as usual when I walked in. No one noticed how late I was, or that my eyes were red and puffy from crying. No one noticed me wince as I walked toward my bedroom. Tears rolled down my cheeks as I considered what to do next. I made up my mind that I would never tell anyone what happened; it was my own stupid fault for missing the bus. But then I thought about Orlando, my first boyfriend, a first-crush relationship. We went to different schools, so rarely saw each other, but we talked on the phone for hours every day. We dreamed that one day we'd grow up and get married and would be each other's "firsts." How would I break the news to him that I was no longer dream-worthy? I called my cousin who set us up. She called an older cousin—who called my mother.

My parents burst into my room to grill me on what happened. I couldn't bring myself to admit that I'd missed the bus or was stupid enough to willingly get in a stranger's truck. My father, filled with misplaced rage charged at me, fist clenched, and punched the side of my head. New pain exploded atop my earlier trauma. Instantly numbed, I flew back onto the daybed behind me and blacked out. The next sound I heard was my own wail, seemingly separate from my body. In the doorway of the room, I could see blurry figures arguing—or fighting. I wasn't sure which. Dad had often been abusive to mom, but he had never laid a hand on us. Regret washed over me—regret for my mother's abuse, regret for telling, regret for making my dad lose control. Poor dad, I thought. This is my fault.

The two men who stole my innocence would be found, convicted, and sent to jail. It didn't matter; the damage could not be reversed. Within weeks, my life was a shadow of what it had been. I'd lost everything. Orlando and I broke it off. Somehow kids at school found out, and my closest friends called me on a three-way conversation and asked me if it "felt good." A therapist suggested that I not return to the school I loved, which also meant losing the TV show. Every interaction with my family was weighted in shame and awkwardness. Dad couldn't even look at me. I couldn't bear to look at myself in the mirror. I was a stained intruder living in my grandmother's former room. This Ebonie didn't belong in her sweet room. This Ebonie didn't belong anywhere.

Home became oppressive, so I ran away. Often. The first time I ran, I felt a sense of relief, like somehow the street was more fitting for the girl I was now. Once innocent, fun-loving and full of hope, I was now damaged. There was no shortage of men willing to exploit a 13-year-old girl needing a place to stay. Sometimes I'd be convinced to return home when they grew tired of hiding me, other times I was found by police and released to my parents. As my folks tried to cope with my behavior, they enrolled me in a private religious school. Soon an employee pulled me into a revulsive sexual tryst she had set up with some sailors. Evil pounces quickly on the vulnerable; my self-destruction was compounding.

One winter morning, I stumbled on a letter my dad wrote my mom. "We cannot allow her to destroy our family. She has to go!" I felt the nausea of ingesting these words. Any sense of belonging was severed in that moment. I decided to leave for good. Before I could execute my plan, my mother pretended I had a doctor's appointment and instead of arriving my pediatrician's office, we arrived at the Psychiatric Institute of Washington, where I was committed.

After about two weeks I was allowed to participate in my own treatment. My therapists rewarded my progress by telling me I would be granted my first visitation. I began hoping my parents might forgive me for what I had put them through, for missing the bus, messing everything up, and that, somehow, I could be accepted into the family again.

On visitation day I was allowed to wear regular clothes and prettied my hair the best I could. I sat longingly on the edge of my bed, waiting for them to arrive as the first hour passed. Several times I got up to see if they were making their way down the hallway with the other parents. Finally, I heard footsteps approach my room. It was my therapist, but my parents were not with her. She'd come to report that they'd decided they weren't ready to come yet. The sense of abandonment was unbearable, and I began to wail like I had on the night my innocence was stolen. The pain felt just as intense, maybe worse. Soon after, I spiked a high temperature, a condition called psychogenic fever, triggered by extreme emotional distress. The orderlies put me in a tub that felt like ice but was probably just cool water. That night I felt like I was going to die. I was inconsolable, so when the fever broke my team determined that I was a danger to myself and locked me in a padded seclusion room.

In this isolation, grief gave way to unanswered screams of anger. Profound loneliness set in. I was too tired to fight anymore. Eventually my reality dawned on me. "I am alone. I have no one. No one loves me, and it's all my fault." I longed for someone, anyone who cared. In the silence I searched my mind for someone on the outside who might notice if I was dead or alive. At that time, in my teenage despair, I came up empty. With no other options, I thought about Jesus.

Church had been a flashpoint between my parents. Mom attended a Pentecostal church and was extremely religious. Legalistic rules dictated TV watching and the length of my sister's nails. Dad was not religious, and resented the control he felt the church had over mom's life. In some ways, Jesus was a troublemaker; more than one physical fight had erupted over something dealing with the church. Eventually they agreed we kids would be dropped off to attend church nearby, while mom traveled into the city for her worship.

Even though I had repeated the "prayer of salvation" a time or two, Jesus didn't make much of a difference to me. But here in this room, if He was real, I needed Him to show up. God began to remind me of all the things I had scarcely paid attention to in service. I felt His presence in inexplicable ways. "He loves me. He is here in this room with me. I am not alone. I am His." It doesn't feel quite accurate to say I met Jesus that night. It feels more right to say He met me where I was, and I gave my life to Him in a padded room.

Our route to a book collaboration is marked by God's signature, authorizing every twist, turn, and crisscrossing of our personal stories. Eb and I met in a post-graduate program I was leading in 2008. Special research and writing projects gave us unexpected opportunities to work together after Ebonie graduated in 2011. After joining other scholars convened by Yale's *Center for Faith and Culture* in 2015 to study joy on behalf of adolescents, I agreed to investigate the role of Sabbath rest as a joy enhancer for adolescents. Eb became my research colleague in this assignment. Near-shameful novices in translating the Fourth Commandment into twenty-first century living with Jesus, we first tackled the topic by reading all we could about

Sabbath rest and habit formations. This fit my career pattern of blending practical theology and social science research.

Then everything changed. One day we were comparing insights and developing the trajectory for a research project proposal. Without warning, our hearts intruded on what had been a comfortable academic head trip. Our pace was irreversibly disrupted. Still is.

We blame Jesus. An inner urgency possesses us both. We thoroughly renounce the generalized and malformational notions of living *for* God in favor of simply, joyfully, restfully, and continually living *with* God.[28] Such a change pulls us first of all into God's deep grace; that's where we'll acquire the identity transfusion we've desperately needed. As we retrieve the best version of ourselves, we want to leave nothing to chance. The notion of personal choice *must* be a factor in this joy journey. But before we declare what we *should* do, there are a few realities beyond our control that need to be understood. At this stage in the book, we lack some crucial info; we're like eagle chicks who don't yet understand gravity or wind currents or—I'm not exactly sure what else since I've never been an eagle chick!

That's where we're headed next. Research about how the brain is energized by joy, our limited capacity to care for others, and the distinctions between efforts we choose to invest in will set us up to explore how social science grit compares favorably to biblical faith. Ultimately, we hope to inhabit practices to feed our love for Jesus and secure our joy.

Joyful Disruptions

Q1. Rank the *Big Three* theological truths from easiest to hardest to believe.

Q2. What in your life feels like it's not "all good?"

Q3. Ask your teens how they experience joy. What surprises you? What caution signs would you raise?

Chapter 3

Brain Joy for Becoming

I have, in the past, half-joked with Ebonie that the reason I asked her to join me in research and writing projects over the years is that I discovered she'd rather die than miss a deadline or fall short of my expectations. What I've learned about the way our brains are wired has led me to regret every version or instance of that utterance.

It's not that I don't highly value Eb's conscientious work ethic. I admire the skills she brings to any assignment. It's just that I may have unwittingly fed the worse of the two options that our brains lean on when we connect to someone else.

Neuroscientists have gained exponential insights with the latest technologies. They can peek in on the brain's innards mid-processing to see what areas light up and what goes dark when presented with stimuli. What we've learned about joy (mostly as a temporary state since experiments are necessarily *here and now* re-creations) leaves us verbose practical theologians speechless in appreciation. Creator God—Who *is* love—imprinted us to mirror His unfailing love. Researchers can watch how the base of our brains initiate neurological impulses that fuel us. When our most important relationships are right, joy floods our minds, releasing the energy that lets us operate at peak performance levels.

There are two distinctly different ways our brains work. These functions, often assigned to one of the brain's two hemispheres, locate the faster control center in the right brain to exert operational control over left brain activity. Nobel prize winner Daniel Kahneman preferred designating the two distinctively different ways our brain operates as systems; one is automatic and the other requires effort.[29] What's not in dispute is how much faster the[30] right side/automatic portions of our brains act; they run operations most of the time by working in the background. There is significant support for the idea that this control center is wired to *work best when we are experiencing relational joy.*[31] In fact, "The brain knows only two ways to generate motivational fuel—a joy bond or a fear bond."[32]

> The critical point between the brain functioning well or starting to fail is where it runs out of joy and begins to run on fear as its motivation... Joy is a renewable energy source that the brain is wired to prefer....
>
> The conclusion of this new science is that relational joy is the natural means for growing a strong, resilient mind. Joy is a natural and sustainable fuel for engagement and the most desirable and powerful of motivating factors in our lives over the long haul."[33]

When we can comfortably relate to those we care about and those with whom we are in immediate contact, the brain's control center pumps fuel into all of its other operations. That fuel, as it turns out, is joy. Remember, it's all good.

Isn't it awesome that the atomic building blocks found throughout creation are, themselves, bonded by the tripled interdependence of protons, neutrons, and electrons? What issued forth from Love at the beginning is also held together now by Love, groaning though it may be in the current state of sin that alienates rather than unites. We live today in hope because Jesus is Lord and will one day reconcile all things, restoring all things to the perfectly fit love relationships that glorify God forever.

Joy is an emotion that involuntarily appears in the fast-track, right hemisphere of the brain when we find ourselves safely attached to what's good. Before our brains form words to shape thoughts, joy is a non-verbal state we have no control over. So, in the most literal sense, joy is not a choice. Choosing is a process that takes place in our brain's left hemisphere, after joy is (or is not) felt. If our fast-track, subconscious radar—updating at six times per second—identifies and assesses that our next encounter poses a threat, we bypass the identity hosting part of our upper-right brain and move toward cramped up, fear-based action on the left side. We fight, take flight, or freeze up. Fear rather than joy guides our decision-making and activity.

Did I unintentionally corrupt my relationship with Ebonie by taking advantage of any *fear* of letting me down she harbored? Was I okay with this kind of bond between us? I now realize I may have been willing to diminish Eb as long as she helped me get things done. Our brains do this math instantly, and we can feel the difference between being valued as someone's useful tool and being loved as a joyful companion.

Shortly before Jesus was arrested, He told His closest followers that it was no longer accurate to call them servants. They were now to enjoy the privileges of friendship, and that would include being trusted as confidants.[34] This was a poignant time in their shared history, one they might have underappreciated in the moment. But Jesus was giving words of explanation to the relationship He'd been upgrading throughout their shared journey. He made clear what He'd steadily revealed while walking the dusty roads of Israel together: joy, not fear and obligation, was the only sufficient basis for their ongoing life together. Later that night, this reframing truth was severely tested when the disciples abandoned Him. As they remembered the shame of their cowardice, Jesus' word of exhilarating promotion must have been more haunting than comforting. From Thursday night until Easter, the promise sat in their hearts' mystery pile where brain attachments operate. They agonized to see Him die with love on His lips for all. Profoundly, He forgave those who crucified Him. But what good would this sacrificial love be for the promised, unrealized intimacy Jesus spoke of? True to His word, Jesus used death to make it so no one ever again needs be separated from the complete and unassailable joy-bond that connects us[35] in a "friendship like no other."[36]

It's. ALL. GOOD!

Ebonie is not the only person I've related to on the basis of their usefulness to me. For years, under the pretext of doing what God had called me to do, my approach with others was intensely mission oriented. I was blind to how devaluing it was to unconsciously tag others as helpful, harmful, or irrelevant to my high and holy purposes. When the Lord graciously showed me that it's impossible to do what He wants while neglecting love, I set my heart on a course correction to *do less so I can be more.* I wince to realize how my default ministry posture was so unfamiliar with the primacy of the love-joy bond God built into our fabric. The neurological light show of my brain scan today is God's grace on display, breeding increasing integrity that mirrors Jesus' love. When attuned by Jesus, we are aligned to joy and can avoid fear.

Book-writing conscious thoughts run a bit slower than my fast-track thoughts, updating at five times per second. My understanding is a *responsive* function to the near constant right-side radar readings. Since words live in the left hemisphere, it's no surprise that's where our focus is located. Think of this as the *narrative,* or *story-constructing* side of our brain. When joy is activated through a good attachment, our *identity* processes live atop this *relational* side of our fast tracks. We experience an awareness that's not yet articulate, operating largely behind the scenes as the final filter from right side to left side brain functions. Because the activity of forming and organizing my thoughts comes as the final step in a process initiated in joy and then aligned to act with identity integrity, to paraphrase Eric Liddell, *When I write, I feel his pleasure.*[37]

Dual-engine brain sequencing assigns the narrative side of our brain to resolve how in the world we can experience the continuous fruit of joy.[38] This shouldn't keep us from wanting the outcome of inextinguishable joy. But certainty is a lie, seeking to control all contingencies. Celebrating a bit too much when situations tip in our favor may make us vulnerable to *conditional* joy; it's how the world, and especially teenagers, understand joy. They believe joy is an emotional state (correct) linked to how well we think things are working out for us at any given moment (not exactly). At any rate, this type of joy is neither durable today nor endurable tomorrow. Fragile and vulnerable to circumstances, it doesn't square with biblical truth.

Isn't this the prevailing perspective most common today? Can you, even now, identify an out-of-balance situation that you hope, when resolved, will help you turn the corner into restful joy? Without much evidentiary detail to support their optimism, adolescents are especially prone to believe things will work out for them. They operate with what David Elkind termed "the myth of invincibility."[39] That's what makes their aimlessness in the splash zone so common.

The Bible speaks insistently of a different kind of joy. "Rejoice always"[40] is a command to those who have moved into an entirely different kind of relationship with the world's circumstances, using our brain's fast-tracking engine.[41] We don't have to ignore the reality that today's excessive blessings may be followed by tomorrow's blindsiding wallop of adversity. But, with the chutzpah of an overmatched action hero who has not yet used her secret weapon, we *choose to see*—via the left-brain narrative engine—beyond how each occasion feels. This is the coaching tip that Jesus' half-brother James offers us across nearly two millennia: "When troubles of any kind come your way, consider it an opportunity for great joy."[42] His advice is a reminder that we should shift our trust (yet again!) to the Lord Jesus, who assures us that we can take heart in the face of our many trials and sorrows "because I have overcome the world."[43] His constant presence, unfailing love, and more-than-enough power is the reason we can be joyful in the now, regardless of the immediacy of our difficulties. This is what it means to live by faith, not by sight. This is what it means to eliminate the "if factor" from our formula for joyful living.

It's okay to celebrate the moments when things work out like we hoped they would. Our Lord Jesus is profoundly present in these victories. But powerful events can overshadow deeper realities. We chase shiny objects too often. As evidenced over and over again in the Old Testament history of Israel, we are inclined to wander away from God. Every time we misattribute a momentary source of joy to the circumstantial wave, God's presence slips out of the spotlight.

My friend Steve learned a month ago that he has cancer. Because of the tsunami of support from friends and family, he can't stop praising God and testifying about the thick peace he enjoys. He confessed to a few of us last night that he's now scratching his head in confusion: Why is it taking this health crisis to surface his deep gratitude?

Jesus shows up when circumstances flip to crush us, beating us down so severely that we beg for God's rescue. When Jesus rose from the dead, His promise to be with us always launched a world-changing reality. From His earliest disciples to believers today, those who know He lives *in them* are freed to transcend the natural system of things.[44] Joy is an inextinguishable possibility because of our "Invisible Rabbi."[45] This is a vibrant faith, authenticated because we've learned to pay attention to what God is doing in and around us. Our stories come alive with exciting, incalculable potential. Teens need adults to show them how this works. And with surprising frequency, parents can recover from their children this way of living in free, simple faith. Anyone who thinks that *states of joy* are all there is must explain the joy some people display when life's circumstantial waves carry the heavy silt of adversity.

On September 12, 1988, Hurricane Gilbert hit Jamaica with a devastating impact. A few months later, I led college students to Montego Bay on a 20-day trip to serve and encourage churches still coping with the wreckage.

We quickly picked up new friends at our work sites, including Charmaigne and her twin sister. Slenderly built, these mocha-skinned 17-year-old girls were lovely, their hair pulled tight atop their heads, neatly held together by pretty bows matching brightly colored dresses. Because of their dancing eyes and brilliant smiles, engaging them was pure delight. Soon, curiosity-fueled story exchanges led to fast-forming friendships. Plans were made to connect as often as possible during our short stay.

During our final team debrief I learned what some of our team had discovered: Charmaigne had a terminal disease—lupus. Her prognosis was death as a young adult. Heaviness surrounded our flight home. Too often, adversity distributes itself unfairly.

Four years later I was back in Jamaica with a smaller group of nine collegians enrolled for a semester abroad. I was the host professor; they blended in with my wife and two young children to become my "ex-pat family" for four months. Thinking about how to introduce them to Jamaican life, I reached out to Charmaigne. She lived near Mandeville where we began our stay. It was not difficult to arrange a rendezvous before any of us even had our first out-of-country laundry experience.

We gathered on a shady porch, pulling rocking chairs into a circle as I introduced my young friend. I explained that my intent was to let them meet a same-aged peer willing to pull back the curtain on her life growing up in Jamaica. It was clear from the start of our conversation that Charmaigne's gracious patience with every uninformed question was a delightful treasure. But lighthearted laughter evaporated instantly when I asked our guest to talk about her terminal disease. The students did not know this was coming.

Carefully choosing her words, my young friend described the life she coped with as a result of living with lupus in a large, poor Jamaican family. I saw how the disease had progressed. Her face was tightly drawn, even as her smile persisted. Scarce resources had led her to forego taking medicine that might extend her life. This was a secret she kept from her family. Younger brothers and sisters treated her cruelly, jealous of the attention their father gave Charmaigne. When she recounted the story of her pre-teen sibling's envious outburst "Just die!" we all choked back sobs.

She saw our sadness and met our misty eyes with a steady gaze and ever-widening smile. Charmaigne leaned in earnestly, hungry to press her point. "You don't understand. I thank God every day for my disease. Without lupus I am very sure that I would not know His love as deeply as I do now." That's when our tears really started flowing. Charmaigne's joy almost defied recognition. She would not be deterred by something as temporal as a terminal disease.

Charmaigne disrupted us with her fierce joy. We were flying down the road of grief, resenting the cruelty that had intruded on this young woman's life so unfairly. Before this seed of discouragement could take root, Charmaigne snatched it with her testimony about intimacy with God. She let us peek into her life and see how durable joy can be. Her authenticity was disruptive. Our brains were in scramble mode, neurons flying between hemispheres, trying to reconcile (story side) the evidence sitting in front of us (relational side) on a Mandeville porch with our beliefs about God's loving goodness.

We each have stories to be discovered; interesting plot developments constantly churn inside. Sometimes hidden from our own view, they are always known by the Lord. This informs 3Story®, Youth for Christ's aptly named ministry strategy.[46] (Briefly, 3Story uses the simplicity of three circles—labeled *God's Story, My Story,* and *Their Story*—to map how our relationships overlap and which direction they seem to be moving. The powerful truth is that we bring the strength (or weakness) of our relationship with God into every other relationship.) Adversity's purpose in our stories might be mysterious to us, but when our faith in God is real, we can relax in the certainty that His love will prevail, and we will know what we need to know in due time. Such trust makes peace and joy possible, even when the state of any "third circle" relationship is impoverished. Why? Because My Story and God's Story are in harmony, and joy spills over from this most important relationship with God so **"It's all good"** and "it is well with my soul."

Charmaigne's adversity revealed the true extent of her faith. How important is authentic faith to young people? Ebonie chased that question with her son:

My teenage son Caleb is generally happy and genial. He's a great student, has close friends, plays the drums, is active at church and loves reading, music, gaming, and parkour. But during this year's "Back to School" youth group night, Caleb hinted that something was amiss. Teaching from Galatians 5 about the fruit of the Spirit, I asked the group. "Which fruit of the Spirit seems most elusive to you?" Caleb's response was unexpected, given his typically easygoing demeanor. He was having trouble with joy and peace. Suppressing my motherly angst, I pressed him with youth pastor skills to clarify. "It's hard to distinguish laziness from peace. I think when I am looking for peace, I'm actually just being lazy, and that affects my joy."

Caleb's transparency continued to reveal his mix of confusing spiritual desires: "I want to spend time with Jesus— but then I don't want to spend time with Jesus." He thinks about Jesus a lot. At times the focus is on what he should be doing as a "good Christian kid." Sometimes he just wishes he could recapture intimate times with the Lord—like the way he felt on the Mexico mission trip. But "doing 'Jesus-stuff' doesn't feel as enticing and relaxing as listening to music" during free time. And music seems too distracting. The song "Addict with a Pen" captures his frustration.[47] Caleb interprets the song as a prayer to God. The lyrics read like a journal entry.

Despite his search to find meaning he feels a gnawing void of what he needs most. He desperately wants the living water that will revive his faith, but instead he finds a desert. God feels out of reach. Too many Christian teens have grown accustomed to this kind of anxiety-ridden life-pace. Distanced from God, they're still thirsty.

Students who broke through with Jesus at summer camp lose their enthusiasm in the months or weeks after returning home. Youth pastors wonder if these students had a real encounter with God. What if this post-camp uncertainty is actually joy's wooing, a "longing for what we already have?"[48] It's crucial they discover how contentment with Jesus—what Caleb understood as peace—is their only reliable source of joy.

Easier said than done.

The pace of life to which young people have grown accustomed has become the sand they're trudging through. It's difficult to focus attentively on loving Jesus when we're crazy busy. There are time bandits afoot, stealing an average of three and a half hours from teens each night for homework alone. Sports, extracurriculars, part-time jobs, and endless social obligations also demand their share of minutes. Young people average 9 hours per day consuming media.[49] They're also tricked into angst by their approach to "down time." Mark Buchanan assesses leisure today as a demanding slave master, more likely to drain us than replenish us.[50]

The constant striving for rewards that fail to satisfy is a human dilemma before it's technology problem. We ignore what God has made available to us all along, as the invitation from Isaiah reveals:

> Come, all you who are thirsty, come to the waters; and you who have no money, come, buy and eat! Come, buy wine and milk without money and without cost. Why spend money on what is not bread, and your labor on what does

> not satisfy? Listen, listen to me, and eat what is good, and
> you will delight in the richest of fare.[51]

In spite of God's plea for them to freely feast on and delight in
Him for glorious living, the Israelites endlessly labored for what
does not satisfy, trapped in wasted efforts, stuck in mud-sucking
maintenance, bereft of delight—like too many teens.

How can we help adolescents to know Christ as an inexhaustible
well of joy from which they can constantly drink? To become
lovingly enjoined to Him? The task is not only mission-worthy for
youth pastors, but it's also a mom's desperate quest.

A finding from the National Study of Youth and Religion
is that most of America's Christian young people have a faith
that looks very little like historical orthodoxy.[52] It is vague and
flimsy, mis-casting God as a distant deity who issues life's moral
parameters and is ultimately responsible for their happiness.
This hardly matches the authentic faith that launched the most
transformational movement the world has ever seen.

The first followers of Jesus Christ were world changers. Their
clarity of passion is unmatched by almost all of us who follow
Christ today. They could draw upon the profound experience of
being *with Jesus*. For the better part of two years, every aspect
of their brains was engaged to make *Jesus Himself* the object of
their passion. It was their privilege to practice being with Jesus
continuously.

Striving to connect, paying careful attention, and responding
quickly are all functions of the conscious, narrative side of our
brains. We apply our best efforts to a life-defining relationship
with our loving God. Notice the brain loop-back in this process.
The super-fast relational side of our subconscious enjoys the

constant presence of God and then awakens us to informed, energized, and grace-directed behavior.

The scientific breakthroughs letting us see brain processing are astounding. As it turns out, the apostle Paul was inspired by the Holy Spirit to describe the duality of our brain functions two millennia ago. How well does the following prayer reflect the mystery of *narrative* operations that are fueled by the joy sent from the *relational* operations?

> May you experience the love of Christ, though it is too great to understand fully. Then you will be made complete with all the fullness of life and power that comes from God.[53]

Joyful Disruptions

Q1. Describe the last time you felt joy before you understood why.

Q2. Who is someone you feel joy with as soon as they look at you?

Q3. When are teens most vulnerable to conditional joy? When are you?

CHAPTER 4

RESTLESS IN THE SHALLOWS

Traffic in the Washington DC area, where Ebonie lives, is unruly. Survival requires patience, a pre-dawn start, and a really good interactive GPS, like *Waze*. A community-based navigation app, *Waze* draws upon real time traffic input from other drivers to guide users along the fastest route to their destination. In any given work week, *Waze* may suggest five different routes. But veterans trust the system. The community possesses beehive-like intelligence, offering outstanding counsel. When *Waze* novices are told to take back roads and unfamiliar paths, they find it hard to trust the directions. Our brains assume that since the shortest *distance* between two places is a straight line, this must also be true for the *time* we spend in travel, too. It's not, as Brandon learned.

A 25-year-old with a new job in downtown DC, instead of using *Waze*, one day Brandon decided to drive the most direct route to his destination. Having abandoned the app that had served him well, he was almost an hour late to work.

While sitting in bumper-to-bumper traffic, God laid Matthew 6:33 on Brandon's heart. Eugene Peterson's *The Message* paraphrase expresses it this way: "Steep your life in God-reality, God-initiative, God-provisions. Don't worry about missing out.

You'll find all your everyday human concerns will be met." Could Brandon give *Waze*-like attentiveness to the promptings of God's Spirit?

When God's voice is more prominent than any other option, we can relax. Trust. As with *Waze*, this is a reciprocal relationship. We abide with Jesus while He abides in us. Alternative options are frustrating and fruitless; they also make us restless. Our anxious efforts will leave us creeping along familiar traffic pathways. "Apart from me," Jesus warns, "you can do nothing."[54] But those who persist in abiding in Christ will be impressed by the gift of *durable* joy they receive.

Given what we know about the brain's involuntary and constant radar hunt for joyful connections—experienced as subconscious feelings that energize us—in what sense can we consider durable joy to be a choice? Both the Philippians and the Thessalonians were exhorted to rejoice always.[55] Why would God issue such commands if joy is beyond our control?

Fruit naturally identifies us, just like it does trees. Jesus made this clear in His teaching.[56] Paul named nine ingredients in the fruit salad of what we can expect when the Holy Spirit transforms us.[57] Whatever we produce will not come from our own exertions. After all, we don't ever hear an apple tree groaning to give birth.

But maybe you didn't realize that each of the nine characteristics listed by Paul as the fruit of the Spirit is *also* issued as a directive we must choose to obey. Or perhaps you forgot Jesus' closing instructions to His most trusted allies before His arrest included the command to *abide in Him* so they can bear fruit impossible to self-generate.[58]

We are genuinely conflicted about trying hard to love God with all our heart, soul, mind, and strength. The American way is industrious; we were raised to believe in work that earns a fair reward. Is it any surprise that this lens on relationships, especially how we connect with God, pollutes our understanding and fails to carry us into the deep mystery of grace? Thinking about aimlessness might lead you to agree that others are *being lost doing lots.* But we're on the verge of an even greater threat to joy among religious people: the restlessness that comes from *doing this to be that.*

What's true for us applies exponentially to teens. If we're going to soak in God's grace, we will need to disrupt our pace. God is not difficult to locate, nor are His gifts in scarce supply. In fact, it's just the opposite. We're like insatiable sponges. Even if our soaking saturates us and we constantly return for more after being squeezed out, we will never exhaust the limits of God's grace. But we prefer quick rinse-offs in God's showers of blessing to the luxuriant bubble baths He's prepared for us. There's something messed up in us that needs to be disrupted. We've succumbed to a life-pace that robs us of soul-marinating joy. We lack a "*Waze*" type of trust in God.

Unintentional living treats time like an ocean wave that, every once in a while, delights us with states of joy dropped on us while we're splashing around the surface, doing whatever we do. Some escape this aimlessness by adopting the possibility of strategic living, exposing them to "under the surface" beauty. A few snorkeling lessons, a little practice, and the right gear opens up a different set of options while time's waves pound away. Random circumstances need not define us if we've got the dedication and focus to work hard and improve. The way we see time deserves to be reckoned with.

But hyper-vigilant obsession to become effective descends on those bent on law-keeping as a way of life. Paul urged the

Galatians not to fall into this trap from which they'd been liberated by Christ.[59] Loveless duty is a taskmaster breeding restlessness.

Restlessness is an apt descriptor for contemporary life. It's a natural joy thief, injecting our days with unproductive anxiety. Adolescents seem especially vulnerable. They are inundated with endless demands on their time, some of which are inflicted upon them as conditions of success. Some requests for their minutes masquerade as leisure, but they often contribute to their restlessness. Social media is *supposed* to be relaxing and fun, but studies show the opposite may be true. The Fifth Annual National Stress and Wellbeing Survey, conducted in Australia in 2015, found that FOMO—or *fear of missing out*—elevates anxiety levels in teens and may contribute to depression. In fact, the fear of being separated from a mobile device has become so pervasive that scientists are studying *nomophobia* as descriptive of the anxiety felt when we our lose sense of being conveniently and constantly connected, especially to other people or information.[60] Jonathan Haidt's research summary starkly concluded our high-tech world has changed the circuitry for children, leading to adolescent social anxiety due to time spent on phones or staring at screens rather than interacting or simply playing together.[61]

While adolescents aren't alone in their phone addictions, their intensity of phone use has conferred upon them the dubious label of *screenagers*.[62] Adults in America are not exempt; nomophobia affects 66% of us.[63]

To make matters worse, FOMO is a downward spiral. Adolescents who participate on more social media platforms in an attempt to combat FOMO are at higher risks for depression and anxiety.[64] Teens themselves are beginning to recognize this. Sixty percent of 13- to 17-year-olds think they spend too much time on their cell phones, but simply can't self-regulate.[65]

Quite a quandary, isn't it? Teens need adults to show them how to escape restlessness and join Jesus in grateful joy, but evidence suggests we're as likely to be casualties to restlessness ourselves as we try to offer help. We are untrained rescue swimmers with good hearts but a lousy strategy. Or is it our incessant search for strategic solutions that disqualifies us?

Social scientists have given us reliable measures for joyful life experiences. They've also concluded that a *trait of joy* is distinctively different from stabbing *states of joy*.[66] Answers to self-report questions can reveal a character quality, or *trait*, by focusing on the consistency of joy in one's life. One item, for instance, invites respondents to agree or disagree with whether they can rejoice when in the middle of difficulty. This is one of 16 such test items making up the Dispositional Joy Scale (DJS). The DJS reliably measures something not quite the same in our human experience as what's found in responses to the State Joy Scale, an 11-item scale that invites respondents to reflect on their past week only.[67]

How are we to make sense of these two different types of observable joy? Try this analogy. We can easily differentiate between loving someone and a sexual encounter that leads to euphoria. The first, at its best, is durable. The second is fleeting. We rightly expect and aspire to loving relationships that are consistent and persevere through adversity. But we don't expect the same from sexual activity. When people pursue sex hoping that it will lead to love, their choices soon enough reveal their wisdom, or lack of wisdom. Biblical teaching about love and sex offers an alternate explanation for the forces at work. When we seek to love our spouse well, the sex that follows is deeply fulfilling.

Prevailing joy is more like dispositional, or trait joy than it is like state joy. It is more like love than sex. Ecstasy is an unsustainable human experience, however profound. In a similar way, state joy is a welcome gift with a shelf life; we can be grateful for each moment it lasts. Unsurprisingly, researchers have found that dispositions of gratitude positively relate to both states and traits of joy. The thankful are also joyful. They have mindsets that help them experience states of joy and gratitude more often in daily life.[68] We consider thankfulness and joy as an inseparable correlation bundle. Both are choices derived from mindfulness. What we notice matters. (And by the way, we can't remember what we failed to notice in the first place.)[69]

Durable joy is a formidable challenge for all of us. Adults who love teens know far too well the difficulty of taking young people somewhere we've never been. Is it even possible without possessing the *dispositional trait* of joy? Eb's story pressed us to weigh the consequential importance of this question.

The Adverse Childhood Experiences (ACE) scale is a 10-question measure that forecasts future health and well-being based on what happened in a young person's life before they turned 18. Developed by insurance giant Keyser Permanente, this highly reliable instrument is now used by the Centers for Disease Control. Any scoring of four or more suggests someone is at considerably higher risk in adult major health categories. Nearly one third of the more than a hundred participants in our research who completed the ACE questionnaire fell into this category. Ebonie's score is "5." Jesus revealed Himself to her during a shockingly deep dive into unfamiliar territory.

Very seldom do the scripts from our old ways flip so pervasively that there's no residue of the damage left behind. Meeting Jesus begins our transformation. Growing to enjoy

His constant companionship is a journey of grace few of us are naturally prepared for. After Eb met Christ while isolated as a 13-year-old in the Psychiatric Institute, she stayed there for two more months. Not sure of much, she knew she was grateful for Jesus' intervention. That led her into an eager adolescent "debt payoff" strategy. She wanted to prove her worth.

Like too many Western young people formed in restless cultures of uber-intense productivity, Eb was left alone to translate her new relationship with Jesus into her way of life. Unfortunately, good role models were scarce. Her mom worked hard for God in a religious way, but severity and duty had been and were her faith brand. Eb lived with her grandparents during the week, but they were only nominal church goers. When she and her siblings followed an upbeat former Sunday School teacher to church in a nearby school cafeteria, Eb figured out a service pathway she could throw herself into. Teaching kids and singing on the praise team helped her become a "good girl" for Jesus.

These activities aligned with her youthful, simple code of morality. No more would she run away. She would be faithful to one boyfriend by limiting her sexual activity to only him (at the time, a guy five years older than she). Getting good grades, participating in school extracurricular activities, and being respectful to her grandparents rounded out Ebonie's profile of being "good."

Without being able to name it as such, Eb had begun to relate to Jesus on a *quid pro quo* basis. She was stockpiling grace and tracking how each "good-girl-for-God" accomplishment added to her burgeoning goodness bank account. The restlessness of her former life took on a freshly scrubbed face, in part because, in spite of her efforts, she never felt "good enough." The gap between God's padded cell rescue and what Eb did to end up in that predicament was a constant indictment. How many young people walk away from a faith they experience as more demanding than liberating? Eb didn't, in spite of her trauma-induced confusion.

Things turned for Eb when she met Clay. He was a sharp guy: kind, gentle, witty, easy going, and attractive. Significantly, Clay was still a virgin, a choice he made as a result of being raised in a Christ-loving home. Their comfortable friendship grew into love, and a proposal followed. When she said "yes," Eb felt like she was undeserving Gomer agreeing to marry God's servant, Hosea. What's more, by her own calculations, this signaled that her efforts to become a good girl may have paid off. She felt like she was on solid footing with God—as long as she kept working.

Many of us think of grace as God's comfort food. Whatever else is going on, however cold and blustery the day, the Lord's grilled cheese sandwiches and tomato soup will make us feel better. But how does grace operate when the way we relate to God actually misdirects us? Too many kids live in the snorkeling world of restless faith, briefly glimpsing what was impossible to see above the surface. Snorkelers can only go so deep and stay underwater so long, no matter how carefully they pace their breathing. They self-regulate. Without knowing better, they imagine that this is the faith deal they signed up for. But they have yet to get acquainted with God's heart and, worse, are too busy *doing for* the Lord to know what they're missing.

This is a very real possibility. Jesus described people who will claim they did plenty of good things and therefore deserve to be with Him through eternity. Our Lord's counter to their claims haunts them forever: "I never knew you."[70] If we don't know God's grace, we don't know Jesus.

Ebonie was profoundly rescued by Jesus, but she was also woefully unaware of how God wants a relationship with Him to work. Lots of us get so stuck in max effort mode that our focus shifts to what we can or should do rather than what Jesus has done. The love that fuels obedience contorts into never-ending performance standards with self-destructive tendencies. On such harmful pathways, grace sometimes shows up as an unwelcome intrusion. It takes a while for us to see such disruptions as gifts. But as severe as they may be, that's exactly what they are. The next part of Eb's story reveals just how audacious God's grace can be when that's what we need.

She was living righteously for God, bolstered in her efforts by a truly good man. Clay enlisted in the Air Force and soon the young couple was living in Japan. Ebonie worked at an off-base Christian school and chipped away at her college degree during evenings. Marital bliss was real, in part because jobs were good and the adventure exciting. Eb's state of joy was near constant. Then Clay got sick. Really sick.

It happened suddenly, while Clay was stateside going through two weeks of training for his new Special Ops role. Stomach complaints from thousands of miles away failed to prepare Eb for what she saw when she greeted him at the terminal back in Japan. Clay's slender, 6'3" frame was disfigured by a horribly distended stomach. He looked like he was nine months pregnant. They rushed to the base hospital emergency room, running lots of tests over a number of days and dealing with a liver that was shutting down, though they did not know it at the time. The decision was made to Medevac him to a USA hospital, and the young couple lived at Walter Reed for the next two months before his liver disease was diagnosed. How did it come about? Doctors didn't know. But they knew that it was ravaging Clay's body at lightning speed. Drug treatments to slow down the progression were quickly instituted.

Something snapped in Eb when her husband's medical specialist, with sorrow in his eyes, said, "Clay has three years—if you're lucky." The thought of becoming a 26-year-old widow led Ebonie to depression—and then to bad theological math. She had been so good, but now Eb's soul whispered another message, insistently factoring all of her guilty past into the equation. Eb was to be blamed. God had not forgiven her, she didn't deserve Clay, and now her husband was being punished for Ebonie's sins. She tried to barter with God, her life for Clay's; then she slipped into depression. Her husband tried to console her until one day, quite out of character, he snapped at her, "QUIT ACTING LIKE I'M DEAD AND START TRUSTING GOD!" As Eb recalls:

His words jolted me. Clay rarely raised his voice, but I needed a radical disruption. His challenge to "start trusting God" pierced my soul in a life-altering way. Jesus was calling me to something beyond "grace for good behavior." This was a Deep Truth moment, like my padded room experience. To survive what was ahead, I needed to truly know the Jesus who met me in my cell when I was most desperate. I instinctively realized I had to go into uncomfortable depths to grow this relationship with Jesus. Without feeling at all prepared, I resolved to go there.

Relentless productivity is an American way of life. We believe good efforts should always be rewarded. When this mindset infects relationships, especially our relationship with God, we unwittingly shoot for usefulness or effectiveness as emblems of the good life. Youth ministers support such efforts, in part because their church parents want their kids to experience the American dream. Both groups are unaware that their short-sighted collusion may cause actual long-term damage. Adolescents peek below the surface and decide, with a little focused effort, they can enjoy snorkeling. Their less-than-deep faith works for them. Until, as was true for Ebonie, it doesn't.

Exerting effort with God is a precision-focused dance of grace. Ebonie got off on the wrong foot. But I also spent years being out of step in my relationship with God. Ironically, they were very productive youth ministry years.

I'll do my best to describe my experience without coming off as too weird. Hundreds of us were gathered at a Youth For Christ national staff conference where David Bryant was leading us in a concert of prayer. At some point during the ebb and flow of the various directed activities, I slipped off on my own. It wasn't that I physically moved away from my seat between Larry and Luther, but I may as well have. Jesus and I were getting some solo time in the midst of a crowd. As I gave Him my full attention I felt, simultaneously, His overwhelming affection for me and acutely self-conscious. A piercing conviction pressed in—I was missing something.

First, I was sitting in a state of silly-grin joy with Jesus. Just relaxing with Him, perfectly content to hang out. Then I began to get fidgety. As I noticed this, I also saw that my agitated state didn't escape the Lord's attention. He asked me what was going on. I replied that I didn't know but hoped He could help me figure it out. Apparently, that was enough of an invitation for Jesus to usher me into a deep, unfamiliar place. He wanted to show me a limp in my spiritual walk that needed healing. I was a seasoned snorkeler—though this metaphor wasn't part of my understanding at the time. Jesus wanted to introduce me to scuba depths and engage unfamiliar—maybe scary—ways of being with Him.

I always felt closest to Christ when I was doing good things for Him. To me, this was perfectly sensible. It obeyed Jesus' teaching on the night He was betrayed: If you love me, obey me.[71] But now, with my silly grin no longer evident, I realized my eagerness to do the next thing for Him was masking my discomfort over simply being still with Jesus.

In a flash, the Lord reminded me of the terrier dog, Mandy, we'd once owned. Our first married home was on the edge of a farmer's mill. Rodents were everywhere, but Mandy had some great dog ninja skills. One spring, the snow melted away to uncover 11 dead rats near our front door. Mandy had killed these varmints and proudly dragged them for presentation to me, her beloved master. I started to sob quietly while I sat between Larry and Luther. The Jesus-directed flashback hit home forcefully. However well-intentioned I was in living *for* Him, my misdirected way of life was Mandy-esque and it needed correction. Jesus wanted me to live *with* Him. As someone deeply formed by Youth *for* Christ this would require new learning.

The lyrics of Graham Kendrick's song, *Knowing You Jesus*,[72] began to bubble up within me. The first stanza and chorus repeated themselves over and over again, gaining a foothold in my heart that still exists today. It is a musical testimony of Paul's "renouncement" in Philippians 3. But—and I can't stress this enough—*I didn't know the song!* I have no memory of hearing the song before that YFC event. Maybe this is simply more evidence of the mysterious way the brain works that we're admiring in this book. All I know is that this is the most intimate experience I've ever had with the Lord.

Jesus, the *Invisible Rabbi*, has been tutoring me in this new way of life with Him for more than two decades. He is lovingly disruptive. As a high-achieving snorkeler, I'm inclined to try harder to gain the results I want. When the problems I encounter are really important—as is almost everything in an outreach mission to lost and spiritually clueless young people—urgency is usually affixed to my efforts. During most weeks my default strategy can be described as "Hurry! Try harder!" And the task is so daunting that there is never a week where everything that needed to get done got done.

As if this isn't demanding enough, I have a tough time accepting anything less than an "A+" on my work. Some people have said, "If it ain't broke, don't fix it." I've long lived by the credo, "If it ain't perfect, make it better." Add a dash of insistent excellence to my natural inner voice and *then* ...

Then realize how highly valued I may be to any ministry organization precisely *because* I can get a lot of things done with excellence and efficiency. My learning was going to require swimming against the current, or so I thought. As it turns out, when you dive deep enough, the current is no problem.

Over ten years ago, I made a career move that was a bit perplexing, even to me. I left my position as a fully-tenured professor at a Christian university to rejoin Youth for Christ in a national leadership role. There were a few factors at work in this decision. But chief among them was the gnawing certainty that the most important thing Jesus wanted me to do was guard my heart.[73] Somehow this shift in employment was going to help me accomplish this. Please don't infer anything about this abrupt shake up other than it was God's clear leading for me. As Jesus made convincingly clear to Peter on the shores of Lake Galilee, His plans for me are not necessarily His plans for anyone else.[74]

Deep diving with Jesus has led me into deeply treasured parts of my identity, tugging me into the best version of myself. I'm learning to relax within His perfect pace and enjoy His constant companionship. At the foundational core of the new man I'm becoming after nearly 50 years of walking with Christ is this truth: *Faithfulness with Jesus is enough.* This conviction wars against the lies lodged in my soul about trying harder and achieving more, falsehoods that breed restlessness. Like Ebonie, I am being delivered from the curse of never doing enough. Woe to all of us who depend on our exertions *for* God to deliver authentic rest or joy.

I'm glad God's grace is so comforting and His sovereignty impeccable. Otherwise, I'd want to race back in time and try some "do-overs." Young Dave ministered to plenty of teens in the fun splash zone. I coaxed them into introductory relationships with Jesus where they could catch a glimpse into the depth of what they could be. We snorkeled together. But I offered no cure for restlessness because I was moving too fast, on a mission from God. With no small degree of angst, I realize I was unacquainted with the deep-water diving Jesus wanted to take me on.

I wish I knew then what I'm learning now. Resting with Jesus is the real deal.

Eager to escape restlessness, many of our teens will "mostly" hear the gospel and jump into God-related activities. Their joy is of the *state* quality, a payday for their strenuous efforts to become good. It's not much different from the satisfaction we all get when some work project is completed. This is no small motivator. Lots of people chase such outcomes in our highly productive culture. But when youth ministry and church parents collude to settle for "good girl, good boy" indicators of effectiveness, we are injecting our own flawed formulae into the relational equation God created us for. Ultimately—eventually—our young people may discover that restlessness still rules their hearts, and they will walk away, unacquainted with Jesus' companionship on a joyful journey into their identity. The alarms have sounded throughout the American church, as it seems a million kids a year are doing just that.[75] Some teens, of course, are content to keep up the ruse.

Either way, we adults who love teens have to disrupt something about our way of walking with them.

Joyful Disruptions

Q1. What have you done for God that didn't help you actually know Him better?

Q2. What's the most common source of your "stabs of joy?"

Q3. What are some ways we adults seem to unintentionally teach teens they need to "earn" God's grace?

CHAPTER 5

DISRUPTIVE FRIEND OR FOE

O nly a month after my college graduation in 1976, I was ecstatic about how quickly my new ministry assignment with Youth for Christ was coming together. It had everything to do with one young man: Dave Stein. We hit it off as soon as we pulled out of the parking lot headed for a five-day backpacking trip in the Smokies. Dave was winsome, earnest, and openly enthusiastic about hearing what I was going to say about God when we were on the trail.

Before we finished our Cades Cove hiking loop, Dave decided he was going to join me as an all-in follower of Jesus Christ. I was freshly scrubbed, 22 years old, and ready to conquer the world through youth ministry. Dave was only five years younger, a white kid from a loving blue-collar family, about to enter his senior year at Elmhurst High School. He was also president elect of the student body and co-captain of the football team. On the Saturday we returned, Dave hunted down his best friend Troi, a black kid from the projects who was vice-president of the student body and the football co-captain. By the time they were done rehashing the trip, Troi was convinced. He, too, was going to become a Christ follower.

This was the summer before I was to be married. With my fiancé an hour away and no other social life to speak of, I spent a lot of time with the guys. We quickly became bonded buddies. Endless discussions about Jesus and the Bible were fueled by bottomless bags of potato chips. One afternoon we spent hours developing our own version of a parable about integrity. We implicitly knew we were making a pact to live by what we crafted. Our three weeks together in the summer of 1976 were rich, intense, and memorable, as life-giving as any I have ever experienced.

And then—tragedy.

Five hours away at rookie staff training, I got the stunning news that both Dave and Troi were electrocuted while trying to unearth and remove a flagpole. Dave was killed instantly; Troi spent months in a hospital burn unit. With accusations in my heart, I cried out to God. None of this made sense to me. The trilogy of biblical truth we wrote about in Chapter 2 were, at that time, beliefs largely untested by experience. *God is Love?* I said this often enough while speaking in front of teens. *Jesus is Lord?* Yup, I even sported a leather belt from my earlier Jesus Movement days that had this imprint. *It's ALL good?* An easy question to get right on a test. But this grief upended me. Losing my newest close friend banished these three truths to await further scrutiny in my brain's left hemisphere.

After my sobs exhausted me, I paused to listen and seemed to hear this response from God: "Have I ever let you down before, Dave?" As soon as I mumbled "no" to the Lord, He hit my soul squarely with this plain and simple whisper: "Then trust me now." I clung to that exchange. God's assertion felt more true as a promise than the vivid pain I felt in the moment. It remains to this day—almost 50 years later—an immense moment for me. A mountain of faith appeared to change the shape of my life's flat landscape.

If I were hosting you on a walk through my faith stories as if they were museum displays, there would be no more significant exhibit in our tour than the experiences I shared with Dave Stein and Troi Lee so many years ago. This personal test of God's promise-keeping trustworthiness rattled my foundation.

Each year of ministry in the Elmhurst community for the next four years I met someone new who shared how their own life was changed as a result of connecting with Dave during the near month he walked with Jesus on Earth. Every encounter was unanticipated. They felt like notes of hope smuggled into my heart by God Himself, reminding me that He *redeems whatever He allows.*[76]

As Troi healed, we shared painful membership in a two-person club. He lived in my house for a time. Heartache multiplied when his younger brother drowned in a pool just before his grandmother who raised him also passed away. We often walked a trail near the YFC office talking about our buddy Dave and how we missed him. After a few years, Troi moved away to invest in young men referred from the juvenile court and share his story of hope in Jesus. When he was only 29, he died of a stroke; the doctors thought his untimely death was probably a latent result of his flag-pole accident more than a decade earlier, when 20,000 volts ran through his body.

I believe God. When the Bible says I ought to "rejoice always,"[77] I conclude that there is a promise of possibility embedded in this command. This conviction survived the core sifting I experienced as a 22-year-old. God met me, offered me His companionship, and asked me to abandon my need to understand what He's doing and to trust him. I did. I do.

Immediately following the Hebrews 11 Faith Hall of Fame list are these two verses:

> Therefore, since we are surrounded by such a huge crowd of witnesses to the life of faith, let us strip off every weight that slows us down, especially the sin that so easily trips us up. And let us run with endurance the race God has set before us. We do this by keeping our eyes on Jesus, the champion who initiates and perfects our faith. Because of the joy awaiting him, he endured the cross, disregarding its shame. Now he is seated in the place of honor beside God's throne.[78]

To this day I am encouraged by the thought of Dave and Troi in the company of Jesus, cheering me on. But I have missed them. True allies into faith's adventurous deep waters are not easy to come by. We should prayerfully seek them out. Whenever we gain the benefit of their partnership, we should thank God for them.

If we're *really on top of our appreciation game,* we can applaud God for the way He made us to enjoy others. It's *really* not good for us to be alone.[79] Thanking the Lord for brains that constantly scan and search for joyful connections with others is important for us introverts to do, while extroverts like Ebonie crazy dance in celebration.

Our brains were calibrated by God to be energized by socio-developmental power. This is especially true for adolescents. We need the social support of a few friends to make major changes. Our attachment centers crave the joy of connectivity to unleash our true selves for good living.

When sociologist Christian Smith started to leak findings from the National Study of Youth and Religion (NSYR) ahead of his landmark publication,[80] the buzz began to build among scholars invested in youth ministry. These data established a baseline of reliability that defines what we understand about young people and faith. Numerous further studies continue to explore and expand on the treasures of the NSYR.[81] Princeton's Kenda Creasy Dean observed from this research that too many young people have a faith fit for the duration of high school; it won't endure beyond their graduation.[82] Her cautions have been echoed in numerous places.

Our cultural upheaval[83] bewilders Christ-loving parents who care deeply about transmitting faith to their teens. We've become obsessed with the need for personal expression[84] where powerful social currents stress test our authenticity [85] and the only way to be true to oneself is to act "outwardly in accordance with one's inward feelings."[86]

These uncharted waters justify the concerns of parents who seek to grow their children's faith. More than a decade after excavating teen religiosity, sociologists Christian Smith and Adam Adamczyk undertook a study about the contour of current parental challenges. They observed that the cultural support parents experience for ensuring their kids meet school-life obligations is tethered to a widely held expectation that this journey is crucial for a good life. Such support does not exist for faith transmission efforts. In fact, the opposite seems to be true. In our hyper-autonomy society parents are skittish about doing much more than wordlessly modeling their faith. Explanations that young people need to make sense of a faith-based worldview are too often rarities. Research describes parents who hope winsome exposure is enough to pass along the faith. Too many fear that, by pushing faith too hard, they might drive their children away. Trend data reveals that this adopted benign socialization strategy is not working.[87]

When Smith's first findings from the NSYR were published 20 years ago, another book—employing a different empirical discovery method—rocked the youth ministry world. Chap Clark made a case that[88] has shaped research Ebonie and I have done, leading us to agree that in spite of receiving unprecedented resources aimed at their well-being, young people feel systemically abandoned and isolated by adults. Further, they have built an underworld of peer relationships to cope with this deep hurt.

Curious to explore what may be an underacknowledged keystone factor in faith formation, we designed a research study to explore the capacity-limited relational environment of young people. Large sample surveys weren't going to satisfy us. Those data felt vulnerable to "noise" (a term unpacked by Nobel laureate Daniel Kahneman in his book by the same title explaining how largely unknown factors inhibit the reliability of our judgments) because young people were asked to make summary conclusions about everyone with whom they had shared faith-based experiences.[89] We decided to probe about what teens had shared with *particular* friends. But how many friends should we ask about?

Since his original study in 1995, Oxford anthropologist Robin Dunbar has shed light on how humans operate with relationship capacity limitations.[90] Rooted in the anatomy of our brains, we cannot care for an unlimited number of people (*caring* is measured by emotional closeness and frequency of connection). "Dunbar's Number" explains that we can manage the ebb and flow of 150 friendships at a time. These are distributed within four concentric circles that reflect various intensities of demand. Inside the largest circle of 150 meaningful relationships, 50 are good friends, 15 are in our close friend category, and five are intimates. Those 15 close friends constitute a "sympathy ring": *We invest 60% of all our social interaction time with them.*

Jesus' exemplary pattern seemed to leverage the neo-cortex relational capacity limitations Dunbar has described. Convinced His incarnational mission was perfectly designed to embrace a human body, I experience wonder-filled praise. God's master plan to reconcile all things was embedded in Jesus' brief, but intense, relationships with invited followers. It's not hard to see Dunbar's relationship circles of 5•15•50•150 reflected in the access Jesus granted His various companions. Only in friendship could Jesus' closest disciples be privy to and grasp otherwise hidden, but crucial, truths about enjoying life with God. The brain's habit-forming processes (later to be discussed) further suggest why our 15 closest relationships can powerfully influence the way we understand and follow Jesus. Those we spend the most time with provide us with social cues that shape our routines for engaging God and our world.[91] It's easy to see how relationships settle into grooves that either exclude or include normal conversations about Jesus Christ as the radical focus of life.

In the summer of 1976, I shared brief, but intense, friendships with Dave and Troi where Jesus dominated our conversational life. They were intimates for a season, easily within a circle of my 15 most important relationships at that time.

A study of how close relationships form young people as Christ followers needs to account for the distinction between *exemplars* and *mentors,* both of whom can be *models* of influence. Ebonie's dinner table discussion with her own two teens probed this topic:

"Random question," I injected to the family chatter over a spaghetti dinner one evening. "What adults in our church make you want to have a deeper relationship with Jesus?" Getting ahead of this possibility (or shielding myself from a letdown!) I stipulated that their answers couldn't name me or their dad. Their responses were swift and in sync. "Ms. Jenny" and "Ms. Loretta."

Not really surprised by their answers, I pressed for more. "Who else?" Pause. Extended pause. Eventually Caleb announced he gave up, paving the way for Lily to also concede.

It bothered me that too few candidates came to mind. My kids have grown up in our church and have known many of the adults in it for most of their lives. Plenty among our congregants have faith I admire, but they failed to meet my teens' sniff test. I nominated a few of them, hoping my name-tossing would stir Lily and Caleb to admit they had simply overlooked these saints of God. Nope. No other adults made their short list. I pressed, "So, are you saying these adults don't have authentic faith?"

Whether they sensed a fight coming or that I might burst into tears, I don't know. But my two kiddos quickly clarified that, while there were lots of adults in the church who likely had strong faith, they weren't appealing. Only Ms. Jenny and Ms. Loretta inspired them to want to go deeper with Jesus.

Ms. Jenny is the favorite of every child that passes through her nursery or elementary Sunday School class. She and her husband Jimmy are known for simple faith and devotion to the work of the church. To be in Ms. Jenny's class is to experience God's wonderland. She invests her whole heart in every VBS or Christmas play and has a way of making every child feel special. When she's not with the children, she can usually be found on the riding mower tending the church lawn or fixing up something in the building. Yet no task overshadowed her sense of worship while serving. My kids knew the difference. She was an informal mentor to many, including Caleb, teaching them to mow the church acres in a perfect pattern, leaving all the clippings in one small area to be raked.

Surprisingly, it was Ms. Jenny's vulnerability that made her so influential in Caleb's mind. She had a rough few years, caring for her ill mother until her mother's passing. Too soon thereafter she learned her husband had cancer. A difficult year later, Jimmy died. Jenny didn't hide her grief from the young people in our church. Rather than disappear into her sorrow, she allowed them to journey with her in her weakness, loving them all along the way. Our teens saw her tears. Jenny did her best to share how God was helping her through the pain. She asked older teens to help her with tasks that Jimmy once had performed, spicing shared work times with conversations about love, faith, and gratitude. Caleb summed up why she got his vote by stating simply, "Ms. Jenny doesn't quit." Her brokenness was visible, but so was her deep abiding relationship with Jesus. This was so much more than any Sunday School lesson.

"Ms. Loretta just don't care!" Lily quipped to explain in a nutshell why her faith hero was worth imitating. We all laughed, knowing exactly what she meant. Ms. Loretta worships God without inhibition. In a church that seems to prize "propriety" during worship, she's not afraid to shout God's praises or let herself be expressively overcome with his goodness. She is one of our founding members, the first African American to break the color barrier at our Southern Baptist Church. Daughter of an illiterate farmer, Ms. Loretta grew up in Jim-Crow-era South Carolina. She's a "church mother" at heart, or maybe she's just a mother at heart. For many years she worked in Title 1 schools as a classroom aide, where it was common for her to bring a meal for a child who didn't seem to have enough in his lunch box or to take a sweater home to fix a button. Her teen-loving reach is legendary in our community, as reported by more than a few adults who return to thank her—all marked by her unforgettable care.

Ms. Loretta sees what's good in every child and tries to truly know each one that God places in her path. She discovers and honors their stories, declaring how God has been present in them. She once reminded Lily about the day she came to our church after my sister's violent gun death landed her in my family and the church's. Loretta recounted the first time Lily gave her a hug and repeated the way Lily's first words signaled breakthroughs over the defenses she'd constructed from her early trauma. This history led to the present, where she celebrated Lily's grades in school, her driver's license, her cello solo, or any other praiseworthy achievement she could think of. Usually, Ms. Loretta ends these with an exuberant "God shed His amazing grace!" And then, as if made freshly aware of this incredible truth, she might burst into a rousing rendition of the song, all-out praise, or tearful gratitude. She expresses what Dr. Richelle White characterizes as the principle embedded in the Zulu greeting "*Sawubona*," which is to say, "I see you as God created you."[92]

Both of these ladies met five of the six classic criteria most likely to make models influential.[93] Ms. Jenny was emotionally transparent (1) while providing explanations about why she behaved as she did (2), especially in the face of tragic loss. Both have been consistent in their faith over time (3), representing the best of the faith community (4) in a variety of situations (5). In fact, if they were Lily and Caleb's age (6) each of the six factors would have been met. It's helpful to think of these as *faith authenticators*, available (or not) to every teen in watching distance, available for dinner-table reflection.

The parable Dave, Troi, and I conjured up during that fateful summer actually squares pretty well with how our brains reckon with the influence of models. We called it the "Camera's Eye." Imagine translucent skin flaps hiding tiny cameras in our foreheads, powered by our heartbeats. These are like video recording machines switched "on" whenever we're conscious. Test it yourself: think of the first person you greeted on your last Sunday morning in church. If the parable we generated holds true, that simple cue invited your brain to retrieve the archived "film footage" you've collected on that person. Those you've known for some time have *lots* of video files in storage, and they were *all* summoned to "on-demand readiness" when you read a simple sentence directing you to recall what you have in your memory.

Many of us would appreciate editorial access to clean up the film footage others have collected on us over the years. Long before we became technologically vulnerable to intrusive phone recordings and social media postings, we were personally exposed to those who spent time in our presence. Each one has a different set of video files in *their brain archives*, labeled with our name and stored without our approval. Sometimes their camera angle is skewed by their own biases or their inability to capture the entire story. This, too, doesn't matter. Regardless of how unfair we think their montage might be, it is what it is. The "Camera's Eye" is always recording. And since we have no control over the footage someone else accumulates under our good name, the best way to affect how others think of us is to live above reproach. Easier said than done, right? By the way, we suspect there's *huge* brain warehousing space dedicated to family memories!

Models may or may not know when they're being watched. Certainly, there is no excuse for parents to be ignorant of the example they are setting for their kids. The proverb that "more is caught than taught" applies to what's most important to us.

Parents are reminded of this by another bromide: "Children learn what they live." The non-formal shaping of models extends far beyond something we *do well*. Rather it testifies to *who we are*, revealing us to be whole persons of integrity or those who let their roles compromise and fracture their identity. It's wise to assume someone's "Camera's Eye" is almost always pointed in our direction. Sometimes the "cameras" whir at a distance, recording our behaviors, sending huge data files to those watching for further reflection at some future date.

Observed and admired, *exemplars* are models who aren't likely to be listed among our 15 closest relationships. In one study, we found adolescent urban indigenous ministry leaders credited extended family members as exemplars who inspired them to first trust Christ. But the teens also named distinctive *mentors* with whom they interacted, crediting these adults for growing and developing them as Christian leaders.[94] While parents are naturally positioned to be religious exemplars, Smith and Adamczyk suggest that not enough of them are active faith mentors, and their general parenting styles are significant factors. Those with permissive, authoritarian, or disengaged parenting styles will be stymied, while those who communicate clear boundaries in the context of carefully cultivated and warm relationships are most effective in passing on the faith to their children.[95]

The "Camera's Eye" captures footage from models who are exemplars and also archives files collected from interactions with mentors. Loving relationships—as provided by Ms. Jenny and Ms. Loretta—include the proximity impact of mentors. For adversity-familiar urban adolescents, faith mentors also encouraged bold leadership.[96]

As Ebonie described the way her spaghetti dinner conversation unfolded, I became fascinated to hear how hard it was for her kids to lock down authentic and inspiring faith models. One explanation (always) is that genuine faith heroes are simply too scarce. Perhaps we adults think our authenticity is self-evident or believe it's a private heart affair, beyond the lens of any "Camera's Eye."

Our authentic selves aren't always—or easily—known to us, let alone others. Fair or not, the "Camera's Eye" does not guarantee our stories will accurately be understood by others. But God is fully aware of every portion of our story, including horrific episodes that send us into shadows of shame and guilt. To actually *become* authentic in faith, our stories need a fully transformational conversion experience.

Significant parental presence notwithstanding, are teens bereft of the mentor-models from *any* sector of their lives that fortify them to thrive in Christ? All of this piqued our curiosity as Ebonie and I undertook research that would let us collect 161 teen stories and study their 15 busiest relational traffic patterns—a number presumably accounting for 60% of all their social interactions. We are convinced that faith influence is significantly carried by those who move in and out of our most important relationship circle, and it would be unwise to assume these complex networks are not fluid or do not include people outside of our family circles.[97] The term "relational authority" seems well-suited to describe what we hoped to find.[98] Our investigation gathered over 12,000 distinct pieces of information from 2,019 index cards representing the closest active relationships identified by these particular young people.

What we learned was sobering. Each index card represented experiences shared in a particular relationship with an adult or peer. As we combed through the data, we realized that each card also fell within one of four different "relational profiles." The two extremes are worth noting here. A relationship we labeled "HERO" meant that this was a person with whom the teen had talked about Jesus, prayed repeatedly together, discussed how to apply the Bible, *and* observed something helpful about following Jesus. HERO relationships may or may not have included a church connection. A first glance at the summary data encouraged us: 26% of all the relationships described by these teens engaged during their church youth group meeting were of the HERO variety. And when adults were named among the young person's top 15, there was a 50% chance they would be HERO types. But 24% of all their most important relationships also fit the "ZERO" profile. Whether these were peers or adults, they shared none of the five faith-supporting experiences.

We picked two unknown teens from the data, naming them "HERO-Heidi" and "ZERO-Zoe" to further explain what troubled us most from our findings. Only a year apart in age, both of them *strongly agreed* with all seven of the Christian belief statements. Each of them also had exactly three peer friendships with whom the only feature they reported was that they had shared conversations about Jesus.

That's where their similarities ended. "Zoe" engaged in heartfelt worship *weekly*, a fairly normal routine reflecting the Sunday emphasis of most churches. She also *occasionally* served "others through church," took "time to be alone, read Scripture and listen to God," and initiated "conversation about faith with others." On the other hand, "Heidi" made "heartfelt efforts to worship" and took "time to be alone, read Scripture and listen to God" with *daily* frequency.

The difference between the two teens' 15 relationship profiles was stark. For "Heidi", 8 of the 15 relationships matched the HERO profile; four of these were adults. "Zoe" had NO adults listed among her 15. Further, 9 of her identified peer friendships fit the ZERO profile. In fact, since *no one* among her 15 closest relationships shared her connection to church, "Zoe" was sitting in a ministry room among peers *at the very moment we collected her information not yet influentially bonded to anyone in her youth group.*

Any particular young person may be a "Zoe" or a "Heidi." Anyone's closest friendships are crucial to understanding their story. How can we know them apart from relational practices that include authentic listening?[99] Christ-loving exemplars—inspiring though they may be—are insufficient. Young people need mentor-level investments from adults whose faith in Jesus is the real deal.

The Occam's Razor principle states that the simplest explanation is usually the best one. Our relationships are powerfully influential. Chap Clark warned of how their neglect causes "hurt" among young people.[100] Something about that warning—and plenty of others—has failed to disrupt our faith formation patterns with one another. We aren't breeding teens to be authentic, joyful, deep-diving companions of Jesus. Entrenched in routines, we prioritize beliefs-as-assent or coach try-harder efforts from one another. Unexamined assumptions, *without evidence,* let us imagine these are the onramps to being transformed by Christ. This doesn't seem to be true.

But the right people to partner with in Jesus' joyful companionship can fortify us for deep-diving change in beliefs and lifestyle habits. Creator God built social connectivity into our fabric; our capacity for such relationships is not unlimited.

Reflect on whether humility, selflessness, and forgiveness are common attributes flowing among those in your local church or the families you know best. Each of these are drawn from the indwelling Christ within us and should set us apart from the world around us. In that sense, they counter the influences of culture. Those who embody them are disruptive friends. Are all others disruptive foes?

As we cautioned the participating teens, basic wisdom will compel us to choose carefully those few who get more than half of our social interaction time. Our need to belong is the attachment-seeking base our brains crave. Under the radar, some people slip into our top fifteen circle of care because no one else is claiming that space and sheer frequency of contact makes them important to us.

Recalling that many adolescents feel abandoned and neglected, should we be surprised at this vulnerability? Puberty has newly expanded their brain power; a developmental hunt for their true identity has been awakened. Hungry to belong, they circulate among others, letting their brains' mirror neurons confirm or reject identity options in their search for the right fit.

That's how some who prove to be more foe-like than friendly infiltrate our high-access relationships where 60% of our social interaction takes place. Friends are confidants who know who we are, where we want to go, and invest in our core identities. Foes do the opposite. They often tug us into their wayward spiral, preferring their self-interests to our best interests. We desperately need reliable, operational identities to sort friend from foe.

Grit-as-faith can do the trick.

Joyful Disruptions

Q1. Which of your own "circle of 15" helps you want to love Jesus more?

Q2. Who was a HERO for you? What made them so impactful?

Q3. How do you know when someone could use one or more HEROES?

CHAPTER 6

How Grit Takes Shape

For years Wheaton philosophy professor Arthur Holmes' book, *All Truth Is God's Truth,* has helped embolden Christian scholars to fearlessly pursue research discovery.[101] We can engage in vigorous academic truth-seeking among colleagues in various disciplines who may or may not share their commitment to Jesus Christ as Lord. Not all truth is revealed in the Bible, nor is all truth provable through the scientific method. But one advantage available to Christians is to appreciate how the connective tissue of God's creation will never be self-contradictory. This doesn't mean there aren't conundrums that don't neatly fit our current understanding. But it sanctions *lots* of wonder-full possibilities for integration.

That's why we'd like to suggest that what one social scientist calls "grit" may help us understand what Jesus *really* means by "faith."[102] Please join us in fearless truth-seeking.

What is "grit"? Angela Duckworth's research defines grit as the combination of passion and perseverance.[103] The first tightly focuses our utmost pursuit with singular clarity. The second applies our efforts with insistent persistence, deeply aware that unless we gain what we're chasing, nothing else matters. Jesus appeared to a first century audience obsessed with self-righteous works, inviting upending faith in Him that—to us—looks a lot like grit.

We were initially drawn to explore Duckworth's work because of how it connects to identity, long considered the primary developmental task launched in the teen years. She correctly writes (in our opinion) about how our identity informs the entirety of our character before concluding that grit provides its directional strength because it is derived from identity.[104] Grit as an actionable, well-ordered life flows from the core we know to be true of us.

How did Duckworth come to understand grit? She was asked to aid the enrollment judgments made by military academies, isolating what best predicts high achievement and ultimate graduation. These elite institutions had awarded acceptance to some of the smartest high school students in America. But in the summer boot-camp prior to matriculating, far too many were dropping out.[105] Could admissions officers identify the "it" factor among thousands of 17- to 18-year-old applicants that would give them confidence they were admitting future military officers?

For obvious reasons, finding a *success silver-bullet* is an investment-worthy enterprise. Michael Phelps is the best swimmer in the world—how did that happen and how can we grow more Phelps-like achievers in all walks of life? Then, to entice those of us convinced that all truth is God's truth, how did Jesus leverage grit to unleash a dozen ragtag followers who would change the world?

Duckworth's studies soon allowed her to dismiss the theory that talent alone explains success. Rather, when talent is enjoined to effort, it produces skill, and when skill blends with effort, it produces achievement. This led her to conclude that effort counts twice.[106] But what unleashes the force of such redoubled efforts?

More than uncommon determination, Duckworth concluded that the directionality that drove them was deeply ingrained in their motivational makeup.[107]

Grit's clear passion directs the focus of unwavering effort. When Malcolm Gladwell summarized research around extraordinary achievers, he found this common benchmark: They dedicated ten thousand hours of practice to their single-minded purpose.[108]

As lifelong youth ministers, Ebonie and I recognized the stark contrast of this gritty attribute with what is commonly found among America's Christian young people. Unfair comparison? Maybe. The earliest disciples spent around ten thousand hours hanging with Jesus. He *convinced* them, *converted* them, and ultimately led to them having their identities *consumed* by Him— exactly as He required.[109] Divergent in skills and backgrounds, they concentrated on being with Jesus continuously.

Of course, this was precisely what Jesus intended. From the beginning of His invitation into the special group of Twelve[110] to His final mission assignment for them,[111] Jesus' companionship was paramount. The disciples quickly learned to depend on the *Invisible Rabbi* after Pentecost. This was the observable power source behind Peter and John's miraculous ministry and their courageous defense in front of the Sanhedrin.[112] Jesus had promised never to leave them alone; the indwelling Holy Spirit fulfilled this pledge. Going forward, God's presence in their lives was to be the ongoing and fundamental source of the apostles' life, strength, and prevailing joy.

The faith Jesus instilled in His closest circle of friends was built on granting them an all-access pass to accompany Him. We can trace our own faith lineage to those Christ-chosen ones. A dozen men without a lot in common multiplied a worldwide movement that is wildly and intentionally diverse. The faith Jesus planted in them looks a lot like grit. To the extent that we can enjoy such faith today, it's because enough of God's people have faithfully lived and shared this identical grit for two millennia.

Identical grit? Can you *identify* with that? Isn't this, in fact, the *identity* we are to share with those who have followed Christ since the Holy Spirit's disruptive visitation in a crowded upstairs room during Pentecost years ago? Imagine being among the 120 believers huddled together in Jerusalem to await further instructions for no other reason than because Jesus said so. Like them, we're to reorder our lives around an indisputable first cause: *attending to Jesus.*

My friend Don Talley is 57 years old and has lived longer than any person known to have his particular form of muscular dystrophy. He retired from a long career in Youth for Christ in the summer of 2024. Almost all of those gathering to celebrate him had seen him hold teen audiences spellbound. Weighing less than 100 pounds, holding his head up by clutching the back of his hair with one of his hands while sitting in his wheelchair, his stories are riveting and his comedy fearless. He knows who he is, loves pointing young people to Jesus, and—navigating challenges unimaginable to most of us—Don logged more than a million airline miles to do what God has called him to do.

He once confided to me a crucial moment in his own faith journey. The obvious nature of his disease has sometimes incited well-meaning travel strangers to greet him with offers to pray that God would miraculously heal him. Recalling when Jesus asked the lifelong paralytic if he wanted to be healed,[113] Don often imagined jumping out of his wheelchair and dancing around the airport if the Lord would cure him. After a number of these experiences, Jesus and he squared off. In Don's words, "Jesus healed me of the need to be healed."

That's the gift of grit.

I had hired Don for a national leadership role in Youth for Christ because he thinks outside the box with a fierce commitment to advance the mission. He's a keen-minded ministry strategist. We both value no-nonsense transparency and will innovate to do whatever it takes to reach kids with the gospel. I've loved being in planning meetings with Don. He's proved his effectiveness.

Lots of ministries seem infatuated with effectiveness. In many ways my career resumé is a roadmap for those in hot pursuit of doing great things for the Lord. But as we noted earlier from Skye Jethani, living *for* God is very different from living *with* God. While I first connected with Don when YFC outcome measurements were a shared obsession, we've both learned a better way. A deeper way. He's one who's been convinced, like Eb and I, that *living with God* is the identity code we need to unlock our own gritty faith. Only then can we become the authentic, Christ-sharing models and mentors our young people desperately need. And only as we're super-glued to Jesus can we produce fruit that exceeds effectiveness.

Fruit that includes prevailing joy.

Joyful Disruptions

Q1. What's most likely to distract you from something important?

Q2. If passion is defined by what we think about most, what's yours?

Q3. What would you need to reorder to make Jesus your first cause?

Q4. Thinking of teens—what will make grit hard for them?

CHAPTER 7

GRIT FINDS JOY'S DEPTH

It's not surprising that one of grit's well-researched achievement cousins is a *growth mindset* that welcomes whatever may come—think of a surfer expecting a gnarly ride.[114] Having a growth mindset puts us in a posture of anticipation and readiness. What's coming our way with time's next wave? Skilled surfers hope it's a challenge. Overcoming adversity is a valued opportunity for those with a growth mindset. Teetering infants who are trying to translate *land* coordination into *sand* coordination don't want *anything* to bother them...especially a big 'ol wave. They haven't learned to spin discomfort into growth.

Unintentional living treats time like an ocean wave that is beyond any control, including preparation. What comes at us defines us. Every once in a while, a wave delights by dropping joy on us while we're splashing around in the water, doing whatever we do. But grit raises the possibility of strategic living that acquaints us with "under the surface" beauty. In fact, grit's first move might be to seize control, redirecting effort to gain the benefit we're pursuing. Can pure dedication always deliver when time's waves relentlessly pound away, each one testing our authenticity? We either see time as an opportunity wave or as the fatalistic source of our happiness. The *NSYR* reports that most teens see God as the distant wave-sender. While they might not perfectly mirror this generation's misconception of who the Lord is, the people Jesus was sent to live among were also wrong about knowing God and how He wants to relate to us. If biblical directives hold the promise of what's possible, joy with God is a choice that's readily available to teens and adults anywhere. Or is it?

Let's go to jail to see.

Operated by the Iowa Department of Human Services, the State Training School for Boys serves all 99 counties in the state. With a history that dates back to 1868, it currently houses young men 12–18 years old who were sentenced as delinquents, mostly at the felony level. Those assigned to "Eldora" (a shorthand name derived from the small rural town nearby) engage in clinical and educational programs designed to facilitate their healthy transition back into their communities. When I visited a few years ago, I noticed that there were no walls, gates, or barbwire fences. The rural location is isolated enough to deter would-be escapees and to quickly catch those who attempt to run. The sterile brick, cement, and metal facilities testify to its age and purpose. Eldora was not designed with joyful fellowship in mind.

God, however, always has joyful fellowship in mind. No one falls off His radar of love and hope. Why should we think otherwise of convicted juvenile offenders in Iowa?

When Youth for Christ Juvenile Justice Ministry chaplains Chad Fincham and Chris Henely attended my workshop about multiplying joy during a national staff conference, they started to dream about how the space they had recently been assigned within Eldora's walls might be repurposed. Volunteers then invested sweat labor to maximize the money allotted by the state, giving shape to an enhanced rec room, a relaxed hangout space available for boys who had earned extra privileges through their good behavior. After touring the other antiseptic, controlling institutional buildings of Eldora, when I stepped into this newly renovated space, I quickly choked back tears. These few rooms shouted, "Disrupt the Eldora pace!" to everyone who stepped through the door. They were beautiful, warm, inviting, hopeful. If a picture is worth a thousand words, how eloquent do you think an island of joy is to boys in lockdown regiment every day? Ministry volunteers who were already engaged in loving Eldora's boys doubled down on their efforts. One of them, Ryne, took a $20K pay cut to jump onto the chaplaincy team, without promise of a long-term job. Nearby youth pastor Brad Hillebrand reconnected with DeMar, a young man in lockup, after having previously come alongside his family during a crisis eight years earlier.

Chad and team hoped every boy could appreciate how this special space was set apart *for* them. But they also want the boys to take "space ownership" and recognize how their precious time in the hangout is also set apart *by* them and *with* them. The notion of being "set apart" feeds off the biblical notion of holiness embedded in the Fourth Commandment: "Remember to observe the Sabbath day by keeping it holy."[115]

Eldora represents a different formula for experiencing joy. Instead of seeing joy as an unpredictable gift randomly delivered on our life beach, adult caretakers tried to build it into the reward-earning system for motivated boys in the State Training School. Time must be well-managed—even overcome—for the young men to gain what they want. Knowing what we do about American culture, should this program design surprise anyone?

An effort-to-outcome pathway shapes a vision of the good life with a debilitating bias. Far too many have a blind spot when it comes to control; we believe in ourselves so much that overreach is common. Vaguely spilling over from our "can-do" spirits is the notion that we should be able to control results and bring about our own fulfillment.

But can we?

The environment of a place like Eldora forms boys to trudge dutifully through the day with both eyes and expectations lowered. They become reacquainted with their limitations by being stripped of their right to control their routines and surroundings. But surprises can take place anywhere, and when these young men step across the threshold into a warm space lovingly set apart for them, joy jumps them like the "stabs of joy" C. S. Lewis described.[116] This welcome ambush is the extent of too many joy experiences. What they (and we) may fail to recognize is that such moments are actually friend requests from God. As with the invitation Jesus once offered directly, so the Lord asks us to trust Him to handle the control issues that make us so restless.[117] Joy is a gift He wants to give us continually. It's delivered as a companionship byproduct when we live constantly aware of His presence.

If Chad Fincham's vision was for Eldora's young men's joy to be temporary and space-centric, that would be the end of the story. But there's a fourth component to their dream. They want teens to learn about space with God and prevailing joy that is set apart *in* them. The word describing what they most hope to give the boys is "portable," something they agreed on after their earliest experiences, like the story below.

Brad enjoyed being considered the fun guy in the hangout's music room. But his religious sensibilities were stretched because of the type of music the young men played. One day as some of the guys broke into their own freestyle raps, Brad was torn about whether to ask them to be more respectful with their lyrics. "But the room was full of joy!" he said. Walking in the tension, Brad chose to let the moment go so joy might gain a foothold. As the chaplaincy team debriefed the visit later, they came to realize how much the boys had come to love this set apart space—and how profoundly sad it made them to leave, be escorted back to their cells, and have their thick metal doors slammed shut on them. The team resolved to help the young men end their visits to the rec hall on high notes they could carry with them as they left. *Portable.*

What transpired in Eldora was remarkable. All sorts of volunteers invested time in this ministry of love among delinquent boys in lockup. For example, three elderly ladies taught the teens some old-school card games that are a barrel of laughs. When the State Training School for Boys was audited by the American Correctional Association—a visit to review 350 standards— they observed rec hall activity involving 11 boys for two hours. They were fascinated to watch two tables of boys mixed with grandma-types playing cards together and later reported that they had "never seen anything like the rec hall." Chad marveled at this finding, especially since the guys being observed were among the lowest functioning, immature residents in Eldora— not exactly the chaplains' prize pupils or models of discipline.

From what we learned about Ms. Loretta and Ms. Jenny earlier, we'd expect them to sling cards as the giggles bounced around these young men. Authentic relationships are the context for conversations about Christ and the new life He offers. It's most common for the adults to make the young men aware of chapel programs that can lead to transformational faith discoveries. But Ryne experienced a reversal of this process when Julio, an incarcerated teen, called him out during rec hall time: "When you gonna come join the family?" That's when Ryne decided to enlist with Chad's Eldora chaplaincy team full time, in spite of the hefty pay cut he would take.

Eldora's set-apart space is worth a thousand words to young men who get to soak in God's grace. Like many of us, their first efforts assume that privileges are earned. They trade surface swimming for snorkeling to gain access to greater possibilities. This is how the very notion of grit most often gets our consideration. Strategies of control seek effective results. But Eldora's secret sauce is delivered beyond the earning through surprising relationships of love offered by fun-loving youth pastors, card-dealing old ladies, and dedicated Bible teachers. Joy is most accessible to those who know they aren't in control but learn to trust the One who is. When we discover that the set-apart space for joy with Jesus is actually *in* us, we embrace a new possibility for the good life: it is *portable.*

Experience eventually teaches us what those in lock up quickly discover: there's a lot of life that happens to us that is beyond our control. But when grit grows its growth mindset, we might just start paying closer attention to what gives us joy.

Study the movements of a very young baby. Is it not fascinating to watch tiny arms and legs flail about? Facial muscles search for expression? Her little eyes lock onto something without any hint of recognition until, suddenly, there is? Through all of the early thrashing about, she learns to control her appendages. It's quite a victory when she figures out how to direct her arm, hand, and fingers so she can grab that plastic unicorn dancing on a string above her head. Her earliest development incrementally expands her control through such movement. She becomes coordinated when she is most skilled at controlling her movement.

Too soon (according to mom), she becomes a teenager and faces a totally different challenge. Physical control over her body is no longer enough to reassure her. In fact, changes within her body are co-mingled with threats around her. Her security shrinks as her sense of self becomes increasingly fragile. Whereas her developmental growth had once been measured by gaining control, this once little baby must now cope with a stunning reversal. Maturity requires that she deals with the shocking reality about how little she actually controls.

Life drags us into coursework around the topic of *control*. We naturally learn what we can do and what exceeds our capability. Entering into a trust relationship with God lets us accept our limitations. Denial is one of sin's trademarks. It curses us with a delusional blind spot, feeding mythical self-determination and breeding restlessness. When teens meet these demands in snorkel waters, they might shrug off the value of trying harder and resurface into the shallows of aimlessness. But when sufficient dissatisfaction sets in, some aspire to double down on their efforts. That's when they get serious about straining to control. Rigorous efforts are praised as self-improvement strategies by those formed in a culture of restless, never-ending productivity.

In spite of overwhelming daily evidence to the contrary, many of us fight hard against the reality that we have control limitations. Our worldviews insist control is necessary to our well-being. Life experiences eventually convince the wise otherwise. Meanwhile, too many of us are too busy intensifying our efforts to notice that, along the way, we've conceded something major. We've come to accept restlessness as a way of life. Our primary coping strategy is concentrated around doing more. We try harder. We strain, grind, procrastinate, and grasp in desperation. Joy, at best, is a momentary state. Sometimes it comes because we earned it, reinforcing our errant master narrative about needing control. Far too prominent in church life, this attitude is also reflected in youth ministries and the advice we offer parents.

Misplaced grit can reinforce this storyline. We all know young people who are obsessed with getting an A without the hint of a minus. The diligent study practices that result in such outcomes are well within the student's control. And most of us average-grade-earning adults are in awe and admiration. But our allocation of grit is a precious heart treasure, and chasing good things keeps us from pursuing the best.

Jesus-directed grit can help us lead young people into durable joy. There's a lot at stake in calibrating grit's object of passion with precision. The Lord's extended tutoring is often needed to lock grit on target. Remember Israel's 40-year wandering in the desert? God's lifetime trust-learning course was introduced in Exodus 16 *before* the Ten Commandments' "reveal party" in Exodus 20. Our discovery through personal experience is real; "faith museum displays" are always formational, no matter what story they are telling.

God is always up to something in the long-term deep that can't be understood from a snorkeler's vantage point. Life's normal waves and currents are distracting influences in need of disruption. This truth helped us see how the heart of Jesus is revealed in His own Sabbath-keeping practices and teaching.

The Pharisees were well-regarded by the people because they tried so much harder than everyone else to be right with God. They were so scrupulously committed to getting the obedience details right they lost sight of what was most important to God. No one could doubt that the religious leaders of Jesus' day were committed to Sabbath-keeping. But their fixation on the Fourth Commandment—and the scores of rules that had evolved to support its practice—had the opposite effect from what God originally intended when he instituted Sabbath as a weekly national habit. The Pharisees were gritty. But they were profoundly off-base in where they aimed their passion. What's more, their influence inflicted restlessness on others.

Jesus' frequent clashes with these regulators of public life disrupted the pace for everyone by insisting that life *with* God is fundamentally different from life *under* God. The experts had masterfully translated religious duty into scripts that would make God predictable.[118] Here's one incident among many:

> One Sabbath day as Jesus was teaching in a synagogue, he saw a woman who had been crippled by an evil spirit. She had been bent double for eighteen years and was unable to stand up straight. When Jesus saw her, he called her over and said, "Dear woman, you are healed of your sickness!" Then he touched her, and instantly she could stand straight. How she praised God!
>
> But the leader in charge of the synagogue was indignant that Jesus had healed her on the Sabbath day. "There are six days of the week for working," he said to the crowd. "Come on those days to be healed, not on the Sabbath."
>
> But the Lord replied, "You hypocrites! Each of you works on the Sabbath day! Don't you untie your ox or your donkey from its stall on the Sabbath and lead it out for water? This dear woman, a daughter of Abraham, has been held in bondage by Satan for eighteen years. Isn't it right that she be released, even on the Sabbath?"
>
> This shamed his enemies, but all the people rejoiced at the wonderful things he did.[119]

Jesus addressed two forms of captivity here. The first obviously targeted the woman's need for healing after being crippled for eighteen years. The second is the Sabbath misrepresentation that kept people from knowing God and His love for them. He immediately pivoted from performing the miracle to talking about how the Kingdom of God is like a tiny mustard seed that grows into a huge nest-worthy tree or the small amount of yeast that makes good bread possible. This was a counter-message to religious legalism.[120]

A life well-ordered *under* God or *for* God assigns efforts to effectiveness categories. It leads to outcome-oriented strategies. For example, though intended to be helpful, the WWJD[121] campaign of the 1990s pulled young people into this sort of snorkel-thinking. Jumping too quickly into Christian behavior makes us vulnerable to the Pharisee's error. Though nothing is wrong with our motives, this way of living devolves into a form of religious godliness that is powerless,[122] slipping and sliding away from the heart of God Who wants, above all else, to be known and loved by us.

Hosea called out this wrong thinking first—maybe best— among Old Testament prophets:

> "Come, let us return to the LORD. He has torn us to pieces; now he will heal us. He has injured us; now he will bandage our wounds. In just a short time he will restore us, so that we may live in his presence. Oh, that we might know the LORD! Let us press on to know him. He will respond to us as surely as the arrival of dawn or the coming of rains in early spring."
>
> "O Israel and Judah, what should I do with you?" asks the LORD. "For your love vanishes like the morning mist and disappears like dew in the sunlight. I sent my prophets to cut you to pieces—to slaughter you with my words, with judgments as inescapable as light.
>
> I want you to show love, not offer sacrifices. I want you to know me more than I want burnt offerings.

But like Adam, you broke my covenant and betrayed my trust."[123]

In spite of his moral failure, David is described as a man after God's own heart.[124] He, too, could discern the difference between religious observance and inward obedience. His contrition after sinning with Bathsheba was real,[125] and he expressed this exemplary faith perspective in another Psalm: "You take no delight in sacrifices or offerings. Now that you have made me listen, I finally understand—you don't require burnt offerings or sin offerings. Then I said, 'Look, I have come. As is written about me in the Scriptures: I take joy in doing your will, my God, for your instructions are written on my heart.'"[126]

This is the language of relationship, of companionship, and intimacy. To know God, to love Him, to enjoy life with Him, properly respectful, but without fear and full of trust; this is constantly disruptive, the nuclear force at work in the center of our "purpose bullseye." David's regret over cutting off the hem of Saul's garment was not wishy-washy leadership; it revealed a heart calibrated for holy sensitivity, honoring his Lord above all else.[127] Confident in his standing with the Lord, he accepted the priests' holy bread when he was hungry, in spite of religious regulations to the contrary.[128] Jesus cited this incident to make a point with the Pharisees.[129] The way David responded to Nathan's pointing out his sins, ironically, reveals the depth of his relationship with God. He sent Uriah to his death and pulled Bathsheba into a dubious future. If we fail to understand the exclusive, gritty focus of his faith, his confessional outpouring will mystify us: "Against you, and you alone, have I sinned; I have done what is evil in your sight."[130]

When our students learn to resist temptation on the basis of calculated ROI (Regret on Investment), they consult their

WWJD bracelets and weigh the consequences of their options. They are satisfied with snorkeling. But when our greatest desire is to please God because we know Him, our hearts align with His. This is the super-power that frees us from sin. It's retrieved by deep diving with God, where His immeasurable love fashions us into Christlikeness. The transformation we experience is so undeniably miraculous that God gets all the credit. And we gain joy with Jesus that is otherworldly, prevailing over any circumstance tossed our way in life's next wave.

When Sabbath rest is a relational effort with our beloved Lord, it's very different from Sabbath keeping for any other reason. We'll explore this in the next chapter. But grit misapplied will make Sabbath one more burden to lay on restless teens. Our brains, optimized by our joyful relationships, have their limits.

Let's revisit Dunbar's relational capacity research through the lens of biblical truth. The tight band led by Jesus Himself two millennia ago set the standard for what can be done. Relationships have power. Perhaps that's why love is God's preeminent strategy. John, a key member of Jesus' team, was so captivated by this attribute he only referred to himself as "the disciple Jesus loved."[131] He certainly knew that Jesus was sent to earth because "God so loved the [entire] world."[132] But love penetrates to our personal depths with such intimate power it can feel like we're the only ones who could possibly receive the Lord's transformational affection. No wonder John is so entangled in love when he writes later in life, concluding succinctly a first truth: "God is love."[133] His version of the Great Commission is the simplest in all the Gospels: "As the Father has sent me, so I am sending you."[134] Sent in love. Sent with love. Sent to love.

Of course, questions arise. Love who? How many? Where? When? Our brains have limitations on how much they can pay attention to, as Kahneman noted.[135] Our capacity for social relationships has boundaries rooted in the size of our brain's neo-cortex. Managing emotional closeness is based upon the frequency of contact needed to sustain such relationships. Earlier we noted that humans have an upper limit of around 150 friendships we can maintain at one time. Some can be categorized as *good friends* (50), some will be *best friends* (15), and a few (5) will be *intimate friends.* The research we earlier described concentrated on the "circle of 15." As Oxford's Dunbar has explained, the number of casual acquaintances and those we recognize by name exceeds the 150 relationships for which we have the capacity to care.[136] Many of us can testify to the impossibility of actually engaging with the inflated number of "friends" in our social media accounts.

Significantly, we cannot love everyone. At least, not in the sense of an ongoing relationship. Our limitations are not a matter of choice any more than our height is. This relational capacity is based on the biological design we have in common. Sometimes we are overwhelmed with the number of people we *could* engage relationally, if only we could find the time. It seems that time is an automatic factor whenever we acknowledge our capacities have limits. God commanded that we remember to keep Sabbath set aside for Him to ensure that—with routine frequency—we acquire His perspective with regard to all of life, including the relationships we invest in. Every moment I entrust to God invites His relational guidance.

What does this mean for our pace-disrupting relationships with Jesus? His love was, at times, wildly discriminatory and intensely focused. It was to his *best* friends that Jesus gave a new commandment—they were to love each other like Jesus had loved them all. He'd picked these 12 over a year earlier to "accompany him" and preach the gospel.[137] Jesus lived within the constraints of human capacity. Dunbar's Number was real enough for Him that He did not grant everyone the frequent access that's necessary for deep emotional bonding. As He tutors us about how we spend our time we can be confident that He "gets it."

For example, John, his brother James, and Peter were all privileged to be in Jesus' inner circle. They alone were invited to witness Jesus raise a little girl from the dead, to see His transfiguration on a mountaintop, and to support Him while He agonized in prayer the night before He was crucified.[138] Even Jesus needed *intimate* friends.

Those who received Jesus' most intense attention benefited from His *formational* love. This sort of love brings about combustive life-change when paired, as it must be, with truth-discoveries in the midst of shared experiences. John, an intimate friend, learned about the love of God up-close and personal. No wonder his gospel uses the word *love* more than all the other gospels combined. This message continued to bear fruit in John's life. By the time he was affectionately referred to as "The Elder" among first-generation Christians, he would emphasize the importance of love so thoroughly into his three short letters that "love" shows up there nearly as much as all of the other gospels combined. John was a witness of Jesus' love, and it formed him to lead with love. Remember? Sent in love. Sent with love. Sent to love.

There is more reason to be hopeful than discouraged. Consider these assets:

1. We were created for loving relationships with God and one another.
2. We experience joy whenever our relationships reinforce our identities.

3. Joy is the fuel that unleashes our best brain performance and endurance.
4. We only have limited attention capacity to devote to relationships.
5. Jesus leveraged this same limitation to launch an eternal kingdom.

The secret lies in our companionship with Jesus. He has the "insider knowledge" we need to make relational time investments. As we establish our lives with Him, we gain joy's constant kickback: loving Him and being loved by Him helps us to actually discover the deepest, truest version of ourselves. When we consider how grit fits in this equation, we are convinced that it translates observable efforts into a joyful companionship with Jesus. We *work at loving Jesus by giving constant attention to His presence with us.*

We apply our gritty best efforts, not to extraordinary achievements, per se, but to a defining relationship with our loving God. This can be especially challenging for Americans in this age, where devotion to things that deliver quick payoffs has been bred into us by our culture.[139] We are raised to be utilitarians. Much deeper than mere *effectiveness* is the kind of identity transformation of which C. S. Lewis speaks, Charmaigne testifies, and Jesus promises. But neither teens nor adults will deep dive into joy unless we are convinced that we need to be rescued from more than aimless surface living. We also need to be delivered from self-directed strategies that are satisfied with a snorkeler's depth and imagine that peeking into God's beauty is sufficient. When someone—be they friend, family, or other folk—lives out an authentic faith, it draws our attention. Don Talley is such an exemplary beacon.

We each have stories, and our telling them often refers to how far we've traveled. Some, like Dave Stein, seemed to grasp immediately what a treasure he had stumbled on with Jesus. Many of us are slow learners. I've been trying to mirror Christ for decades, but I'm not sure if my starting point was an advantage or disadvantage to discovering that being loved with Jesus is more transformational than doing good for Jesus.

Those who are lost are very often unaware of their condition. I was such a clueless kid in 1970. My ability to articulate what was missing in my life was vague, at best. I sincerely thought I was a Christian because of my American roots—I'd been taught in school that the USA was a Christian nation. It was not until I heard the gospel 11 days before my sixteenth birthday that I realized God wanted a personal relationship with me, made possible because of Jesus Christ. A quick inventory of what I had going for me at the time was my version of "counting the cost." I calculated that I had nothing to lose and everything to gain by trusting Jesus with my life. Without fully understanding what I was getting into, I said "yes" to Christ. That pledge has defined my life for more than 50 years.

Jesus' compelling passion for the lost tugs on my heart, personally. He once aimed this teaching at the host of a banquet He was attending: "'When you put on a luncheon or a banquet,' he said, 'don't invite your friends, brothers, relatives, and rich neighbors. For they will invite you back, and that will be your only reward. Instead, invite the poor, the crippled, the lame, and the blind. Then at the resurrection of the righteous, God will reward you for inviting those who could not repay you.'" After He whet the appetite of the crowd with these tasty appetizers, He spelled out exactly where these instructions were headed: "If you want to be my disciple, you must, by comparison hate everyone else—your father and mother, wife and children, brothers and sisters—yes, even your own life. Otherwise, you cannot be my disciple."[140] The crowd was advised to count the cost of following Jesus. So are we.

We cannot back into the conclusion of our second fundamental truth that *Jesus is Lord* without considering the weight of this life-altering confession. Everything changes. Each *relationship* changes when Jesus takes over. We become flavorless, unusable salt if we hedge on our agreement to surrender all of life, including our most precious relationships, to the Lord Jesus. We can't possibly love like Jesus until we die to ourselves like Jesus did.

As we tackled research to understand joy, Eb and I recruited mentor volunteers to learn more about how gritty efforts might benefit from practice habits related to enjoying companionship with Jesus. During that discovery process, 22 different small teams of 18- to 26-year-olds from 13 American cities completed an eight-week experience together. A ten question "Grit with Jesus" survey was part of their initial baseline of work. We also gathered data from Youth for Christ leaders all over the country. Our vault of collected data has 240 surveys. Do these relatively modest efforts support the idea that grit applied to our ongoing relationships with Jesus is a difference-maker?

See what you think.

We developed our "Grit with Jesus" survey patterned after Angela Duckworth's original work.[141] The higher the score, the grittier you are about being in constant contact with Jesus as a way of life—at least that's the target we were shooting for. In one of our subset samples, about one third of the respondents logged scores that favorably compared to Duckworth's assessment of grit among adults, exceeding the scores of about 69% of respondents.[142] Among this grittiest third:

- 44% of their responses to life scenario situations were: "Strongly aware of Jesus' presence, I enjoy steady, quiet conversation with Him." This same choice was made 33% of the time by everyone else.

- 84% of their responses to other life scenario situations were: "I would have inner joy regardless of the situation." This same choice was made 62% of the time by everyone else.

- 53% answered questions revealing they have a *growth mindset.* Only 26% of all others could say the same.

Three of our ten grit items surfaced as especially dependable measures to suggest a group formed around one idea: *the challenge of handling distractions while connecting with Jesus.* Statistically correlated, here they are:

I constantly make new efforts to stay closely connected to Jesus.

It's not uncommon for me to intend to keep my focus on Jesus but get sidetracked throughout the day.

Whatever else is going on I stay alert to Jesus' presence in me.

We've intuited that negotiating with time is a big deal for all who want to enjoy life with Jesus. That's what fascinated us about Sabbath-keeping as introduced by God millennia ago; it's both a pace disruptor and a life regulator. Once a week, we can press the "reset button" to keep from spiraling out of our preferred posture of trusting God completely.

After I received my Ph.D. from Purdue more than 30 years ago, I concentrated research on youth ministry practices. Inquiring minds want to know, right? I've confirmed hunches, debunked the effectiveness of some common practices, and located next-layer insights that help us focus our efforts where they matter most. For instance, my colleagues and I once discovered that the greatest concern among youth ministers in America was that their busyness robbed them of their devotional time.[143] We can see nothing about our contemporary landscape to indicate that harried time conflicts are less concerning than they were twenty years ago. But, while I've gained genuine benefit from research, I've never felt that the scientific method is a universally better way of knowing what's true. The Bible asserts an epistemological wild card that should be considered in our endeavor to navigate life: *the mind of Christ is available for those bonded to Him in loving companionship.*[144]

We adults need the disruptive mind of Christ if teens have a chance at durable joy. Unless parents and caring mentors aim the directional focus of faith-as-grit, chances are young people will be misled into thinking the Christian life is about trying hard to become good boys and girls. Knowing what we know about socialized learning, if families live in purposeless fog, they can't help teens who are stumbling in darkness and unaware that deep joy is even possible. The gaps in our grit focus need to be exposed. Jesus is willing to show all of us with ears to hear and hearts willing to be tutored. He'll be gentle, as He promised.[145] That's a good thing because we seem to be protectively sensitive about the way we spend our time.

We can't imagine actually *growing* grit with Jesus that neglects reckoning how we spend our minutes. As Paul prayed for those to whom he wrote, may you gulp God's grace and grip God's peace as you dive where grit takes you: *into prevailing, deep joy with Jesus.*

Joyful Disruptions

Q1. Which teen self-directed strategies most commonly miss the mark?

Q2. If joy gets *switched on* by being grateful for someone, who comes to mind?

Q3. When was being close to Jesus the only explanation for your joy?

Q4. What would you need to surrender to love like Jesus did?

CHAPTER 8

GRIT IS PACED BY GRACE

From 1819 to 1823, Spanish artist Francisco Goya painted 14 different oil works directly onto the walls of his house. One haunting piece in the dining room was titled *Saturn Devouring His Son*. It's named for the Roman version of Greek mythology's titan *Chronos.*[146] In an instant, observers grasp its meaning and relate to the terrifying portrayal of time hungrily swallowing our lives. Goya's advanced age (over 70) and health problems when he created these fourteen "Black Paintings" reveal a man for whom joy was elusive. *Saturn Devouring His Son* points to time as the culprit. Do you feel the same way?

But that's not how God intends us to experience the minute-by-minute life gift He entrusts to us. Our time on earth is to be cherished. We are invited to steward all of creation, not as hirelings or deputized overseers, but as sons and daughters of a loving Father who wants us to enjoy the family business with Him, sharing both work and relaxation.[147] This is a heart-stopping notion, incredibly profound in its implications. We will not easily get our minds around how to make this relationship work. It only makes sense that to know God in this way will require both dedicated effort and attentive flow.

Flow. It's actually another member of grit's research family tree.[148] "Flow" is described as "being in the zone," like when Kaitlyn Clark can't miss a basketball shot or a jazz musician plays a jaw-dropping riff. It describes optimal performance. Joy comes along for the ride when our gritty double-efforts are rewarded by flow that is, quite literally, otherworldly. That's what we're hunting. That's what Charmaigne represented as her reality while, incredibly, she was being ravaged by lupus.

Remember Duckworth's assertion that effort counts twice for the gritty? It's easy to picture exhausted smiles as a reward for some massive task accomplishment. *Grit* has a quality of onomatopoeia to it, sounding like the *dirt* or *grime* or *sweat* that proves we dug deep into our reservoir of resolve and delivered max exertion. But if Jesus-obsessed grit is an acceptable explanation of biblical faith, our redoubled efforts have to aim squarely at *flowing* with Jesus into joy. We have to learn how to try really hard to gain something we can't gain by trying really hard. It's like being told to "Relax as if your life depended on it."

We've got to learn how grace works.

Note that God's standard hasn't changed at all. We *should* love the Lord with all our heart, soul, mind, and strength. We *should* love our neighbors like we care for ourselves. We *should not* murder, commit adultery, lie, steal, covet, or make an idol of anything that will displace God's rule in our lives. Religious demands that wallop us with too many things we *"should"* do can crush us rather than empower us. It's always seemed to be that way. The Old Testament record offers a thousand pages of evidence that we *can't* do what we know we *should* do.

In countless ways God's chosen people broke God's laws. And though, from our twenty-first century American perspective, the Fourth Commandment may seem a strange member of the Top

Ten list Moses delivered, its violation was a huge deal to *Yahweh*. Why? It was a keystone practice for the relationship God wanted with His chosen nation—a heart-guarding, weekly routine Israel was directed to observe. They were not unaware of either the precision or reason for this command, as seen in Ezekiel's retelling years later:

> I brought them out of Egypt and led them into the wilderness. There I gave them my decrees and regulations so they could find life by keeping them. And I gave them my Sabbath days of rest as a sign between them and me. It was to remind them that I am the LORD, who had set them apart to be holy.[149]

The psalmist urges us to be still for the purpose of knowing God.[150] But sometimes we let grit's original clarity slip off-target. Once Paul met the living Lord, he realized he needed to disavow the misplaced Pharisaical zeal he'd been raised in. Hyper-sensitive vigilance around Law-keeping was one discipline that became "worthless when compared with the infinite value of knowing Christ Jesus my Lord."[151] Clearly the religious effort during Jesus' day was not achieving the singular goal to which it pointed. Paul's prior training had helped him see and show why the righteous "shoulds" of the law could not be met without the grace delivered by Jesus Christ.[152]

Is it any wonder the first believers saw this as "BREAKING: Good News!?" God the Father sent God the Son to live among us, embody the love He wants for us, and die to set us free from the "should-keep-from-sin-but-can't" zombie walk defining us. Jesus' resurrection was and is proof certain that there's a whole new forgiveness deal with God, joining us to a life of joy with Him that lasts forever.

Can you imagine being among those who heard words like these from Jesus' own lips and *then* were reminded of them by the indwelling Holy Spirit after Pentecost? "Are you tired? Worn out? Burned out on religion? Come to me. Get away with me and you'll recover your life. I'll show you how to take a real rest. Walk with me and work with me—watch how I do it. Learn the unforced rhythms of grace. I won't lay anything heavy or ill-fitting on you. Keep company with me and you'll learn to live freely and lightly."[153]

When hopes are realized, joy often shows up. But joy can also be experienced by faith-as-grit. It anticipates the certainty of what we do not yet have in hand. Jesus, "endured the cross, disregarding its shame"[154] for this promised-but-not-yet joy. This may seem like a small distinction, but it represents a life-changing directional calculation. Faith wrongly invested messes up grit's powerful focus, ultimately taking us to a destination that's very different from where we really want to go. Living *with* God leads us on a path that those living *under* or *for* God can't see.

It's hardly effortless to learn how to hear from God in our contemporary noisy world. Has it ever been easy? Recall the anxiety that a nation of escaped slaves felt during their Exodus from Egypt. Israel was second-guessing their decision to abandon their former life; centuries of abusive oppression had messed up their thinking. In spite of the spectacular miracles that made their rescue possible, the notion of trusting either God or Moses, His appointed leader, was still discomforting. Today's culture of productivity might feel endless, but we obviously have more choices than did the slave nation of Israel under Egypt's rule 3500 years ago. There was major learning ahead of them.

The timeline in Exodus reinforces our point. After the Lord God powerfully and miraculously liberated them from their captors, Israel had difficulty *un*learning their old slavery mindset. Restlessness and anxiety had understandably become their way of life. The recent memory of walking through a dry land corridor as the Red Sea parted wasn't enough to relax Israel's skittishness. To build their trust in Him, God made an identity-defining move. He stuck a stick in the spokes of their productivity pace by establishing a law to be observed once a week, every week. "Remember to observe the Sabbath day by keeping it holy."[155]

When compared to the others, this Fourth Commandment certainly seems out of place—unless it's *necessary* for living in faithful obedience to the other nine. Did they—do *we*—require the benefits of a disrupted pace to live in restful companionship with God, as He intends? Certainly, Israel needed an identity reboot. They were no longer restless slaves splashing around to meet life's endless obligations. God chose them, and they needed to see themselves in this light. Now He constantly reminded them of their transformational status from Him: *They were His beloved.* The Lord's unfailing faithfulness means trust is now part of their identity equation.

This school of trust during their trek involved manna. But there was a conditional clause in *Yahweh's* food provision. As Exodus 16 reveals, the Sabbath was to be set apart as a day of rest. The normal rules for food gathering would not apply on this day so God could teach His people how to relax with Him and live without being fearful or anxious about *anything*. As the story unfolds, we realize this lesson was not easily learned. The obligation was dropped on Israel at Mt. Sinai. Discovering "how" needed a 40-year tutorial to squeak by with a passing grade. The idea of a habitual, weekly Sabbath to anchor the identity of God's people is beyond brilliant. It is inspired.

We were designed to enjoy our relationship with Creator God. But this is far too tame to describe what the Bible says is really going on for those stamped with "*imago Dei.*" The Hebrew word *hesed* is used more than 250 times in the Old Testament; it usually describes God's unfailing love. This is a love that refuses to go away, regardless of the pain we cause God through our incessant rebellion. "Relationship" or even "right relationship" is an inadequate descriptor when it comes to love. Our greatest purpose on earth is to enjoy the companionship of our *hesed* God. And when we lose our way, as aimless teens have, God authorizes disruption.

Enjoying restfulness with God and living under His care was a disruptive new way of life to be learned by people who'd been enslaved for centuries. Our *hesed* God instituted a 40-year relationship recovery program. Adam's idyllic life in Eden before banishment is still appealing. The invitation stands to this day: we can live in joyful companionship with our Creator God. The good life spills over from trusting the Lord. If Israel could embrace this relationship and obey God, their lifestyles would testify to other nations that a pace disrupted by God—*with* God—ushers us into the best version of ourselves.

We disrupt the pace so we can see how much more is available than what we gain by thoughtlessly doing what we do. Joy can be a choice. The good life is possible. Teens need our examples to inspire them. If disrupting the pace is crucial to *our* journeys in the adult world, it's doubly so for frenetic teenagers.

I imagine Frank Bell nodding in quiet agreement as he reads this. He busily disrupts the pace of under resourced young people through Elevate in Ferguson, Missouri. His slender build and easy smile are deceiving; Frank is a force to be reckoned with.

We met in February of 2018 because I needed help with a program I would be leading in St. Louis nine months later. Ninety minutes after connecting in the hotel coffee shop, we embraced in a tearful hug.

This is not my normal first-meeting experience. Why the emotional response? We were both touched to recognize God's unmistakable hand at work in bringing us together. And frankly (pun intended), we were overwhelmed to realize Jesus wanted to include us in what He was orchestrating. With inarticulate confidence in God and little else to go by, I declared that somehow, some way, Frank would be part of our program in October. My new friend graciously agreed to my embarrassingly vague terms of engagement.

The phrase, "disrupt the pace" was an off-handed summary Frank came up with over dinner one night. He had been describing how he reacts to high school classroom chaos when teaching about character development. Secure in his own identity with Jesus, he felt at ease to sit in silence when students lurched into noisy distractions. His quiet confidence asserted a calming influence on his class. They soon acquired a routine of self-correction as Frank first gave and then gained respect. What was going on in his mind as he sat in their midst? *Disrupt the pace.*

Jesus' love disrupts the pace always. He does it *with* us in our heart's private rooms. He also does it *through* us when we make ourselves available to Him. Confessing Christ as Lord gives Him permission *anytime* to disrupt our pace. This invitation is mere lip-service if we fail to give Him our attention so we can hear what He wants us to learn. That includes recognizing His voice in the midst of busy, noisy lives.

We earlier referenced the brain science of relational joy and anthropological studies about our relational capacity. I can partially explain connecting with Frank through these lenses. But the heart of the story can't be understood through empirical investigation, however fascinating. Frank and I were instantly bonded to each other because we've each been absorbed by Jesus. Christ's loving companionship is the secret we share.

Expect the unexpected with Jesus. He is disruptive. But we can shrug off the surprises in our schedule with a relaxing posture of trust. Burdens once dense and thick become lighter than air. And one February day in St Louis, new conference plans were born. Our work efforts tangibly *feel* different with Jesus in the mix. Outcomes beyond imagination blow our minds,[156] like when Peter and his fishing crew first met Jesus and let Him handle their business.[157]

Legendary UCLA coach John Wooden inspired a book beyond basketball with his oft-quoted practice tip, *Be Quick—But Don't Hurry!*[158] Sometimes the hurried pace of family members, church friends, or ministry teammates throws off my own preferred life rhythm. When I recognized how impatient I am with others' impatience, I decided not to toss any of the judgment stones I had collected.

There is hidden value stuffed into the time we spend waiting. But it can only be gained by those who leverage the patience given by the Holy Spirit. Ironically, the sooner we learn this truth, the quicker we can benefit from it.

We could counterbalance life's restlessness and show young people how to thrive if we were less anxious. But how? The core solution reflects the relationship with God for which we were created. That's the context in which we should understand Jesus' offer to tutor us when we yoke up with Him. Living with God necessitates personal discovery experiences. We will be restless without such learning, and our joy will lack durability.

Jesus' incarnation shows us how we can relax in such a relationship of trust. Through His death and resurrection, we gain breakthrough access to this new way of life. The Gospels let us peek in on the disciples' learning during the couple of years they were privy to Jesus' constant companionship. What jumps off the pages of the Bible is how often they had to learn from their failures. Eb and I are also on the roster of uncoordinated saints; we're grateful to know the disciples stumbled so often. Strange learning territory leads to regular mistakes, and Jesus' teaching was unlike anything they had heard before.

One memorable teaching-learning incident illustrates the gap we all must navigate. Jesus asked His disciples to board a boat with Him and head to the shore across the lake. To veteran fishermen this simple request was no challenge. Jesus settled into the back of the boat for a relaxing nap. But a fierce storm quickly blew up. Acquainted with this type of weather, the Galileans were panicked enough to awaken Jesus with cries for help. Without breaking a sweat, Jesus rebuked the storm and instantly calmed the wind and waves. Next, He asked the disciples to explain why their hearts were fearful and their faith didn't work. Their response revealed they had much to discover about Jesus and living restfully with Him. His authority is boundless. Their control limitations needed attention. It took a high-drama moment with Jesus to force this reckoning.[159]

The young faith of teens will need reinforcing breakthroughs after they confess Christ is in charge. It becomes possible to enjoy a right relationship with God *only* when we see God for who He is. We should not be tentative about the humility this demands. *Jesus is Lord.* He is not befuddled by any situation that mystifies us. Nor will He be, as "[H]e holds all creation together."[160] *It's all good.* Joy prevails when we rest in the ever-present company of Jesus. Our inability to control what comes our way is a given. Whatever results can be traced from our efforts, however skilled or clumsy they may be, are redeemed by Jesus. Relax. Enjoy. Let go.

Joy is a choice. It shows up as a command of Scripture in 1 Thessalonians 5:16–18, implying a promise that is stunning. We *can* "rejoice always," and so we ought to do so. We can also "give thanks in all situations," so why wouldn't we? Since social science research has reinforced the existing connection between joy and gratitude, perhaps the "meat" of the biblical "sandwich" in this passage deserves consideration. A constant relationship with the ever-present Jesus is also a bumper-sticker-sized verse squeezed between joy and gratitude: "Pray continually."

Continuous prayer reflects being attentive to God's constant companionship. This is a pace disruptor. It brings fresh awareness about who we are so we can beat our chests in enthusiastic discovery. Like a bearded lady, we can belt out our own version of the anthem "This is Me."[161] Identity awareness focuses teens' efforts. It can't be gained by snorkeling because it requires prolonged familiarity with the deep water of their souls, where God's whispers can receive their undivided attention. Such diving needs our help.

God chose the nation of Israel to be His special people. By ordering their lives around His powerful presence and rule, they were to be a light to the nations, revealing that *Yahweh* was the One True God, unrivaled among ancient deities. When things went well, Israel brought glory to God. Unfortunately, much of the Old Testament story reports the failings of Israel to keep God's commands and to instead bring ruin upon themselves by misrepresenting the good name of *Yahweh* in the world. When they lost their way with God, they lost what made them special. And when the Lord rebuked them, punished them for their waywardness, or called them to repent, one focal point was their failed Sabbath practice.

Isaiah attached Sabbath-keeping to the citizenship pathway for eunuchs, foreigners, and outcasts.[162] Jeremiah declared to the splintering nation how important it is to keep the Sabbath.[163] We earlier noted how, from his prophetic post in exile, Ezekiel succinctly retraced why keeping God's commandments—especially Sabbath-observance—was to bless Israel and set them apart as His people. Even though the Israelites were scattered in Babylon, their hope could be realized by seeing God at work in adversity, recalling them back into a right relationship of obedience.[164]

Sabbath-keeping was an identity marker for God's people. It was a weekly habit God established to define them, testifying to the world that their covenant relationship of trust in *Yahweh* made them special. Centuries ago, the apostle Paul urged us to embrace an even more profound identity:

> Since you have been raised to new life with Christ, set your sights on the realities of heaven, where Christ sits in the place of honor at God's right hand. Think about the things of heaven, not the things of earth. For you died to this life, and your real life is hidden with Christ in God. And when Christ, who is your life, is revealed to the whole world, you will share in all his glory.[165]

Research about grit powerfully illuminates why the Fourth Commandment was such a big deal. Integrity flows from identity. Israel was weekly reminded who, and *Whose*, they were. They set aside a day to ensure God's presence was central to their life together. It was the most intentional use of their time in the week, deliberately designed for them to unplug from work and fixate on God's goodness. We have a natural inclination to improve on life or solve problems by adding more.[166] Sabbath-keeping gains through subtraction. Is this a way the Father "prunes the branches that do bear fruit so they will produce even more?"[167]

When we listen to God's voice, He disrupts our obsessive pace of endless productivity. Always *doing* is a crushing burden that causes us to believe we can gain what we want without losing who we are. We can't. The pace of grace is wonderfully counter-intuitive. With Jesus we learn to do less so we can be more.

Sabbath-keeping had this intention.

After Jesus assured listeners that He didn't come to abolish the law but "accomplish [its] purpose,"[168] He intensified expectations. Avoiding murder or adultery isn't entirely what God wants; anger and lust need to be extinguished. In the same way, we see that Jesus isn't calling us back into the really good idea of keeping a weekly Sabbath so much as enjoying His constant, restful, and fruitful companionship. There's no flow like Christ's grace!

Attending to Jesus takes time and effort. It's where we must aim our grit. Whatever needs to get done will get done on time and better than ever, like what the newlyweds in Cana experienced when their celebration wine was miraculously resupplied and upgraded. Grit with Jesus trusts Him with all of our time, all of the relationships we juggle, all of the creative innovations we might need, and all of the responsibilities we carry.

Without a doubt, the world will not mindfully assist us in this passion.

To enjoy continual companionship with Christ, doesn't it make sense to develop and practice habits that elevate this relationship above anything else clamoring for our focus? Those who are most gritty about living with Jesus will do exactly this. Grit cultivates and protects a singular life passion. Too many surface splashers suffer from goal ambiguity. Too many snorkelers fail to find and draw upon the depth of their identity with Jesus.

Seeing the Fourth Commandment as a first-order habit got us wondering about how being transformed by our mind's renewal[169] so "we have the mind of Christ"[170] aligns with our brain's habit-formation processes. First, we become deep-diving apprentices, learning from Jesus' active tutoring. Then we embrace the adventure, ready to dive into depths we've yet to inhabit and get to explore for a lifetime. Discovering the deep, powerful ways with Jesus is crucial to discerning the lies that suck life from us. Families and teens, like Jews enslaved by Pharaoh, have been ensnared by the endless hurry to *do more*. We can *BE more*. Why fantasize about stabs of joy when persistent joy awaits? Let's disrupt our pace. Let's inhabit the grace of grit with Jesus.

Joyful Disruptions

Q1. When do you feel like you are "in the zone" with Jesus?

Q2. The *pace of grace* means you're OK with not being in control— are you? If not, how does that trickle down to the teens you love?

Q3. When did you last welcome God disrupting your normal routine?

Q4. What would change if you trusted Jesus more with your time?

INHALE

GRITTY INNOVATION

"**L**et it travel."

While watching my 13-year-old grandson Brig's baseball game, I heard coaches say to their batters, "Let it travel." This tip was to help the player not swing too early at the incoming pitch. In our post-game debrief, Brig declared his "good swing" needs better timing.

We all do.

Faithfulness with Jesus includes perfect timing. Doing the right thing at the wrong time is not obedience. Carefully listening to the distinctively recognizable voice of Jesus, as all of us "sheep" who have *ears to hear* are coached to do, is crucial to our whole-hearted love for God. Is it even possible to act in perfect, fruit-bearing harmony with Jesus? Not without hearing His Spirit speak up: "SWING NOW!"

We have come to a *deep-breath* moment in our book. Our exploration of Scripture and research in pursuit of joyful, authentic faith has led us to converge on a crucial conviction: *The only grit worthy of our singular passion is the grit that intensifies our intimacy with Jesus.* Too many are surface splashing without grit or deceptively snorkeling in the shallows with misdirected grit. The trait of joy will elude them. The next generation is unimpressed.

The Lord wants each of His beloved to contribute particular work for His one purpose.[171] We're to take swings with Him. Baseball fans know that even the best players swing and miss more often than they hit the ball. How fantastic it is that behind every failed effort, three things are true:

God is love.

Jesus is Lord.

It's all good.

In fact, the whole master plan of our Creator is that, in Christ Jesus our Lord, *everything* is being ultimately worked out for good with—even *through*—our erratic and ill-timed zigzags of faithfulness. *His love never fails!*

We grow fruitful lives as we persist to be with Jesus. Joy comes when our relationship bond is front and center. Forgive my excessive baseball analogizing, but in the very long professional season of game days where personal at-bats are more likely to be bad than good, the grind can be a grueling beat down to staying positive. When faith, hope, and love thrive in our daily lives, it's because the greatest of these (love) has clawed through crusty layers of our hearts, laid claim to our soul's personality, taken over the command center of our minds, and supplied us with unlimited grace-as-strength.

We're about to explore what grit insists on: *HOW to get better.* Brain science about the anatomy and value of habit formation figures into the four practices we commend for our sharply focused grit. But just now—with plenty of our own exhausting swings-and-misses archived in "Camera's Eye" files—we'd like to disrupt the pace of this book-reading journey. Step out of the batter's box and into Jesus' rest. Pause. Remember.

Let love travel ... deeper ... wider ... longer ... higher. That's how waiting with Jesus prepares us for our next at-bat. Each next life-swing can help us grow in God's perfect timing as the Spirit's voice becomes familiar and vividly clear. And in the aftermath of frequent, in-the-moment failures, love's forgiveness awaits, poised to flush the shame and redeem the value we had no idea was possible from that particular experience. *God's love never fails;* **let it travel!** And let the gritty dig in, ready to test inhabited grace at work with Jesus.

CHAPTER 9

GUEST: JESUS-CONNECTED

Our brain's foundational structure confirms that our identity processes live in the brain's fast track and operate behind the scenes. These cruise along inside the brain's gray matter at pretty impressive speeds, with a great deal of adaptive flexibility. But the brain creates opportunities for energy-saving efficiency through habit-forming routines in response to familiar situations. The neuro-highways of such habits are coated with white insulation, a process taking at least a month. Once insulated, the habit cluster operates up to 200 times faster than do our normal, gray matter brain operations.[172]

Most of us have acquired some bad habits coated in white brain matter insulation. They work at 200 times the speed of normal mental activity *against* our desire to love Jesus more and more each day. We need disruptive habits to replace destructive patterns, purging their privileged access to our minds. In partnership with the Holy Spirit, we can unleash our grit for just such a purpose and more. Habits await that will help us "see God more clearly, love him more dearly, follow him more nearly."[173]

Our goal is not to become non-thinking, habitual lovers of God. That defies the very essence of love, doesn't it? Rather, we want to acquire habits that better position us to enjoy the ever-present companionship of Jesus, Lord of Love. Consider this warning:

CAUTION

*Habits can be useful because
our brains ache for efficiency.
But this efficiency lies beneath the
awareness we need to choose love.*

Loving relationships need care lest neglect's slow drift ruins what once was cherished. This distancing sneaks up on those who aren't vigilant. In *A Severe Mercy*, Sheldon Vanauken memorably recounted the resistance that he and his beloved Jean, or "Davy" as she was called in his book, agreed to practice.[174] The warning to warily guard relationships of importance from failed "apartfulness" fits the concern we want to target.

A too-common health condition illustrates how well-aimed habits can help us align a passion for life with Jesus with the resolve to avoid this slide away from union and into separation. Arrhythmia causes the heart to beat with an irregular or abnormal rhythm. In essence, the heart is out of sync. At their worst, arrhythmias can be life threatening. The best treatment is to install a pacemaker, a device that regulates and recalibrates the heartbeat.

The notion of arrhythmia, applied to the rhythm of our relationships, sheds new light on our habits. Anyone who has been married has likely been out of sync with their spouse at one time or another. Sometimes family demands have husbands and wives "passing like two ships in the night." More painful discord can also pop up. Whatever its origin, spouses should make intentional effort to guard against "relationship arrhythmia." At one marriage workshop, the session leader encouraged busy couples to set a weekly date night in their schedule. That time was to be protected with fierce devotion, regardless of what other potential obligations came up. If the day was Wednesday, then all through the beginning of the week, the couple would speak in code about looking forward to "Wednesday." After their special night, they would spend the second half of the week speaking in code about how much they enjoyed "Wednesday." The playful banter surrounding the evening built both excitement and gratitude for their time together.

Weekly date nights can serve like pacemakers, jolting relationships with intimacy. But recalibration is not the only reason for a pacemaker. And "Wednesdays"—even heart-pumping "Wednesdays"—are insufficient to avoid drifting apart. Daily routines of communication and affection are also necessary to help spouses stay aligned. Just as untreated serious heart arrhythmias cause the heart to deteriorate, relationships will inevitably erode when they lack habitual rhythms of love. Out-of-sync marriages send couples apart from one another, unaware of how the smallest, routine inconsistencies are mini-fractures that may eventually weaken the relationship beyond repair.

If, by preferring personal rather than shared interests, we endanger our marriage relationships, does that explain why love's earliest stage of natural, complete abandon becomes vulnerable over time? Especially if intentionality is lacking? Many of us testify about how Jesus' love captivated us as we initially got to know Him. We would rather not talk about how creeping toward separateness might erode our relationship. The risen Christ warned the Ephesian church that—in spite of their persistent and dutiful hard work—failure to love Him or one another as they did at first puts them at risk of losing everything.[175]

Practicing the right habits is a high-stakes, life-size strategy.

The first habit we commend is to leverage the forces of friendship to embolden each other for the challenging journey we share. We are headed down to deep waters where we can be more completely and joyfully disrupted by Jesus. But we're likely starting in the aimlessness of surface living or the restlessness of shallow, misdirected pursuits. Our passion to be with Jesus must prove itself in our willingness to do whatever it takes to reach our goal. Experimentation is worth the effort if improvement can be gained.

In the spring of 2021, inspired by COVID restraints, I decided to try Zooming with a few really busy ministry leaders and youth ministry professors to upgrade our friendship. We'd shared in kingdom work but not necessarily obsessed over Jesus together. My invitation aimed to introduce a fresh element to our relationships and see if we could do so in groups of three tightly focused in four meetings of thirty minutes per week.

By respecting their own busy schedules and honoring the pledge to meet only for thirty minutes, I was trying to learn if a little effort could go a long way. Three people can jump on a Zoom call and each share in five minutes about how Jesus recently met them in a fresh way. Then we can pivot immediately to Spirit-led prayer for one another, allotting another five minutes each to actually engaging the risen Christ together.

To be sure, it's often a joy to extend these conversations, provided we all have the time. But if not, we've managed to talk about Jesus with one another and then talk to Jesus about one another—introducing new shared experiences to what the "Camera's Eye" captures and stores in our brain's storage center.

Having tested this innovation with 18 different duos who agreed to join me, it's now one of my treasured weekly habits. I stumbled onto something more crucial than I had anticipated for my own journey with Jesus. I meet Roger and David weekly on Zoom and have done so for the past three years. Both are busy and travel a lot for their work. That means it's not uncommon for us to move our 9 a.m. Thursday times to another window; that's not a problem when there are only three schedules to align.

More organic than formal, these two guys are among my most trusted allies. They clearly occupy space in my "circle of 15." I don't think of them as an accountability group,[176] per se. But they help me go where I want to go with Jesus by sharing the same gritty direction I am passionate about. When they make time available each week to deep dive, it encourages me to be the man God fashioned me to be. I try to do the same with them. It's important to the brain's joy process that we actually see each other's faces (Zoom!) so our fast-working radar can see how much we love being together. Mirror neurons do this work before any narrative story lines can find words.

Marcus Warner says that being part of such a group is the first step he takes in order to establish a new habit.[177] We all need such identity reinforcements. They remind us to be true to ourselves and sometimes help us reconnect with what drives us. Because they, too, are on a deep-dive quest, we can compare notes about our personal discovery efforts with Jesus. What I love most about my times with Roger and David is when we chat about how we experience Jesus at work in our inner lives. I feel my heart enlarging with Jesus' love during those conversations.

We once labeled this habit "QUEST" because it reflects the doubled-down effort gritty people take to pursue their passion. This squares with Duckworth's research. But we want to be sure not to fall into the same switcheroo trap that Paul warned the Galatians about.

My old self has been crucified with Christ. It is no longer I who live, but Christ lives in me. So, I live in this earthly body by trusting in the Son of God, who loved me and gave himself for me. I do not treat the grace of God as meaningless. For if keeping the law could make us right with God, then there was no need for Christ to die. ... How foolish can you be? After starting your new lives in the Spirit, why are you now trying to become perfect by your own human effort?[178]

If grace isn't central to the habits we form, we will fail to benefit from the Holy Spirit's indwelling presence. When we connect with allies to dive deep, we are simply answering the door Jesus is knocking on to fellowship with Him.[179] And, no matter how much we might busy ourselves to welcome Him into our lives, the good stuff happens when we are his *guests*, and He sets the agenda.[180] By the way, in case it's not clear already, Eb and I enjoy *GUEST* experiences with Jesus, and our own bond has grown through this partnership. We've mostly operated through these same sort of video calls. After we realized that only a third of our time was being dedicated to research and writing task accomplishment, we knew that we had become really important to one another's deep diving with Jesus. All of us adults will need such partners if we're going to show teens we love the Lord with life-defining passion.

Referencing Old Testament standards for sufficient witnesses to confirm truth, Jesus said that two or three of us gathering in His name or agreeing in prayer are enough for Him.[181] He'll come through when your tight posse is pulling together in the same direction. Count on it.

Of course, we sometimes bring "extra exertions" to lend support to God's promises. America is a builder culture. We love things that are bigger, almost certain that more must be better. So naturally we think God will more likely answer us favorably if 150 people pray with us than if we're simply supported by two or three teammates. Behind this lurks a damnable formula: We try to impress God with great effort, so we obligate Him to do our bidding. This is a relationship betrayal, inconsistent with humbly surrendering control to Lord Jesus.

Would you rather have two or three godly people pray with you over an important matter or 150 American Christians? Be careful. 72% of Americans identify themselves as Christians.[182] But only 20% of Americans say that their faith is the most important source of meaning in their lives.[183] If we value dependability, it pays to be picky about our prayer partners.

That's why *GUEST* is such an important habit. Its focus is to partner with just enough people (according to Christ) to help us live faithfully and fruitfully. We obviously were not made to journey alone in life. Even Jesus asked His closest friends to stay with Him while He labored in prayer hours before He was crucified.

Persuasion research indicates we can resist others' influence when we have one true partner to stand with us.[184] Adolescent peer pressure has been mythologized as a bad thing when it's as likely to be positive as it is to be negative; the real influence indicator can be traced through adolescent friendships.[185] Who we spend time with makes a difference in how we think, what's important to us, and how we behave.

For the purposes of the *GUEST* habit, frequency of contact may be more important than the emotional closeness we feel with someone—at least at the start. In a nutshell, find two or three partners eager to experience Jesus' companionship more consistently, then meet at least weekly for Christ-centered encouragement. Be ruthless about guarding the focus of your connection time. Split your 30 minutes about evenly, first by talking *about* Jesus *to* one another and then by talking *to* Jesus *about* one another. It's most important that our partners share our gritty craving to intensify this relationship with God and agree that transparently talking about habit practices will be mutually beneficial. Any *good* friend (think: top 50) with whom we connect daily or weekly who "wants to go there" could become a *GUEST* teammate. If they agree to join you, don't be surprised if they soon move into a closer circle of intimates, those with whom you share 60% of your social interaction.

More extended times are always welcome. But too many of us busily important people don't consider invitations that will intrude too much on our schedules. Thirty minutes can sprinkle salt into a relationship not yet flavored to Jesus' taste. Start simply. Ultimately, tweak this practice to fit you and your *GUEST* partners.

If you're a habit-forming geek (we may be!), you know that what we're suggesting as a weekly routine doesn't have the power of a daily habit. Well-chosen habits leverage the limited capacities of time, thought, and relationships that we all have in common. By making some processes automatic, we conserve energy. Consider how you spend the first few minutes after waking up. Much of that activity is practically thoughtless—a needed rhythm until we jump start our focus. If normal patterns get disrupted, you may more likely forget to do what is otherwise automatic. A middle of the night crisis phone call invokes the need to create a mental checklist, expending precious thought energy so we don't rush out the door without brushing our teeth.

Unlike right beliefs requiring conscious attention, humans calculate how or if we fit with certain people quickly and imperceptibly. Group identities are constantly evaluated as we choose where to belong. Can you identify *habits of interaction* that infuse each of your closest relationships with their own dynamics? Whenever possible, our brains seek to conserve energy by converting gray matter thought routines into white matter super-speedy habit highways. It's too easy for our highly familiar relationships to slip into behavioral ruts that may or may not benefit our grit to live in Christ's joyful presence.

Until three years ago, my routine interactions with Roger and David considerably aimed at whining about our Cubs and Bears, trash-talking during noon basketball or golf (Roger), or giggling about something funny (David is a professional comedian). These patterns settled us into shallow comfort. With respect to the earlier HERO profiles, our considerable "Camera's Eye" archives revealed meager evidence that our relationships were Christ-centric. But we've disrupted our pace such that talking about Jesus is now a normal part of our interaction together. To be perfectly accurate, the habit isn't so much about making weekly time together (it's crucial) as it is about *what we share* inside that space. That's where our brain's autobahn kicks in.

Also, since each person's closest relationships are fluid, life transitions often rearrange who gets most of our attention. Few changes match the dramatic nature of these adjustments as much as that of young people heading off to college—is this a likely correlation for the number of late teens disaffiliating with church? If so, habits like *GUEST* may be the simplest way to curb this crisis. My friendships with David and Roger began when we lived in the same town, but I moved ninety minutes away over a decade ago. The gift of Zoom means that home-church mentors could continue meaningful connections that remind and embolden young people to enjoy Jesus always.

This is probably why family members' status among our closest relationships tends to be more stable over time than peer friendships. Even so, exemplary parental behaviors go only so far; faith transmission requires transparency and words that explain how Christ *in us* guides activity *by us*.[186] Teens dispossessed of clarity about Jesus Christ at the root of their parent's life may vaguely understand faith, but should we be surprised if they're vulnerable to the influence of others in their close relationship circles? Earnest parents anguish daily about whether their Gen Z sons and daughters will return to church—we urge them to personally plunge into Christ's lovingly disruptive ways. Those humble and hungry enough will find it worthwhile to reflect on whether Jesus is or is not front and center inside the interactional dynamics of their fifteen closest relationships. The truly gritty will leave no stone unturned to seek *GUEST* level depth and companionship with Jesus.

As we discovered in the index card research project earlier described, each young person has a story about the profiles of their "circle of 15" that can be evaluated like an investment portfolio. Is close friend influence helpful to those who aspire to radically focus on Christ? Unless caring adults prioritize their shepherding responsibilities to present winsome options in this world's relationship bazaar, the very foundation of Christlike character development in the teens we love may fail to be activated.

"Zoe's" story, mentioned in chapter 5 is haunting. If the net direction of a teen's closest relationships is indifferent—or hostile—to living with Jesus as Lord, the odds are stacked against faith resiliency. Innovation in youth discipleship will be leveraged by relationship shepherds who earn privileged influence through proximity and loving listening. This is the portal through which adults can shape teens' Christ-focused beliefs and practices.

What's at stake is whether we adults are willing to redirect our time, putting first our own deep journey with Jesus. Only then can we see what needs pruned. Too many youth ministers settle comfortably into predictable programmatic routines, neglecting the messy and often intimidating world of teen relationships. Largely uninvited and sometimes unwelcome, we adults must choose nevertheless to selflessly discomfort ourselves if we hope to gain relational authority. What will convince mentors-in-waiting to penetrate the relational environment of young people? We doubt that research data will open hearts yet to be convicted by the Holy Spirit. But we have great hope that the same love that unlocks youth discipleship transformation is also key to deepened authenticity among adults. Innovation flows freely among gritty collaborators. While not explicitly aiming at solving problems beyond the desire to encourage deep diving with Jesus, we should not be surprised if *GUEST* teammates attack other challenges together.

As apprentices of Jesus in a discovery adventure for durable joy, *GUEST* partners are crucial. Ask the Lord for friends with whom you can pray weekly or more. Make Jesus the unquestioned focal point of at least one shared gathering. Watch—and celebrate—when relationships inhabit a new way of engaging one another. Our best friends bring out the best in us; Eb and I think best friends are those we depend on to carry us with them into Jesus' presence. Chances are they'll also love swapping stories about enjoying Jesus while finding more workable habits.

Let's be clear. The habit for us *GUEST* tablemates is to meet together weekly to become more Jesus-connected than we are. It's a heart-triggering opportunity, nothing more. If postured in humility, we open ourselves to the flow of God's grace, grow our grit, and experience joy with Jesus.

Joyful Disruptions

Q1. What routines do you already have that help you stay connected to Jesus? How faithful are you to those habits?

Q2. Name two allies willing to dive with you for gritty joy with Jesus. What's a first step you could take to find two allies if you don't have them?

CHAPTER 10

REST: JESUS-ATTENTIVE

Key question: Will teens acquire grit best through their innovation or by adopting yours? Eb and I have concluded that we adults must balance giving young people enough practical help to encourage their persistence but *not* solve their listening challenge. Paying attention to Jesus is, first and foremost, a matter of desire.

As we introduced this habit to those testing it with young people, we warned that it cannot be private. It's true that identity we will retrieve in the deep with Jesus will be uniquely shaped for our personal understanding.[187] Each of us is one of a kind. But we are also always and forever interdependent. There is no such thing as solo work in the Body of Christ. Rather, we are stitched together by Jesus, the Head, with particular gifts for specific work to be done. When we are faithful contributors to the Church "each part does its own special work, it helps the other parts grow, so that the whole body is healthy and growing and full of love."[188] If we tackle our own assignments from a place of shallow impoverishment in our relationships with Jesus, are we being helpful or hurtful? Our private lives have very public consequences.

This is a crucial biblical principle to understand, consequential in shaping the next habit. *REST* carries unusual status as it swaggers into our consideration. After all, a version of this was once written on a stone tablet by God Himself. The essence of this habit, importantly, must be understood in light of Jesus' life, teaching, triumphant death, and resurrection. We think it's a wise, gritty endeavor to protect an entire day each week for *REST*.

Rest does not come easy to us. Like Israelites in the desert, fear makes us frantic. Imaginary control tempts us to ignore the command. Protecting a day for rest requires courageous trust. We surrender to God that which feels urgent, with the conviction that He will provide perfectly for us.

This habit is especially time targeted. Management consultant Stephen Covey circulated an illustration that's nearly legendary, easily confirmed by home experimentation. Get a large jar, big rocks, pebbles, a bag of sand, and a jug of water. Pour the small items in first and then try to add the big rocks. It won't work. But if the big rocks are first loaded into the jar there's a chance for everything to fit. Covey's lesson is simple enough: first things first.[189]

Sabbath-keeping was God's original idea, a habit intended to help His people keep first things first. Like Covey's effectiveness training, it helps us with time management. It deserves consideration in any debate about useful strategies. But we hope by now you've caught our warning about mere usefulness as a target; that's as deep as snorkelers can get. We need to understand why God commended Sabbath-keeping and Jesus fulfills it. It looks like a habit designed for us to review priorities with enough frequency that correction is not such a herculean task.

Buchanan asserts that our busyness is a thief of what's most important, especially stealing our ability to know God.[190] With grit-induced clarity, we can ask ourselves how much we really care about what we say is important and how does that care show up in our calendars, routines, and habits. If we only care about what Jesus wants for us, do any of the "extra" pebbles matter?

As we frame this *REST* habit, we've chosen not to specify *which* day should be protected, only that it be a consistent day each week. The omission is not an oversight. A year into this journey, Ebonie attended a Passover Seder with a Messianic Jewish couple from her church. The meal shed beautiful light on Jesus, our Passover lamb. The hosts united their Jewish heritage with their love for Jesus as the Messiah. When Eb pressed to understand Sabbath by asking whether the day might be flexible, she learned that—at least to this couple—Saturday was the non-negotiable day for rest. Christians may be similarly attached to Sunday.

Two generations ago, blue laws were commonplace, and stores were not open on Sundays. Those days are long gone. Our culture is not going to protect Sabbath-keeping practices that honor Jesus Christ and safeguard our relationship with Him. It's oriented toward market desire and productivity, hungry to acquire, relentless to accumulate. We won't get cooperation for a society-wide practice in support of our *REST* habit. Should families and youth ministries huddle bravely in sub-cultures of resistance, holding tightly to days set apart for God? How can we make something work for everyone? What's the heart of God about this practice?

Jesus is. When decisions are confusing, let gritty faith guide us into faithful innovation. There are clear rejuvenation benefits to be gained from a weekly day of rest. But that's utilitarian thinking at snorkel depth, a pebble-sized priority. In fact, we can see advocates of this sort of "Sabbath" writing articles in popular magazines near the drugstore checkout. Far more than gaining common-sense life balance and margin, our first concern is to set aside a day for Jesus' deep-diving companionship. Doing so will grow our trust in Him, help us acquire His perspective on the week we just concluded, and take His hope with us into the days ahead.

When possible, *whatever day* is protected for rest should be consistent each week. Much like the rhythmic reset of husband and wife, our hearts function optimally when we can predictably anticipate a day dedicated to practice Jesus-attentiveness. Ruth Haley Burton writes,

> The human being, body, and soul, responds to rhythms and is accustomed to living in rhythms—night and day, three meals a day, the seasons of the year. Part of the restfulness of Sabbath is knowing that it is always coming in the same interval, so that we're not making decisions about it every week. When Sabbath is not observed on the same day every week, it means that we go longer than seven days without a Sabbath, and that is not optimal. After seven days without rest we are at risk of becoming dangerously tired. Because we do not rest, we lose our way. We miss the compass points that would show us where to go, we bypass the nourishment that would give us succor. We miss the joy and love born of effortless delight.[191]

The practical question for this *REST* habit is to understand what activities we should and should not do. Sabbath's reputation is that it is overly concerned with regulations, hardly the *easy yoke* Jesus invites us to wear on the way to experiencing greater rest from our burdens. Carrying weighty obligations makes it difficult to skip into joyful freedom.

We were keen to field test the workability of establishing *REST* as a life habit among tenth graders. This can't be too complicated. Hopefully the strategy below is helpful. If not, please innovate. It's what the gritty do.

Unlike *GUEST* and the other two habits we will suggest, we've given *REST* the additional benefit of being an acronym in hopes of boosting an understanding about how to give clear shape for a day set apart with God.[192] Please don't read these as legalistic regulations; think of them as keys to the map we will use. Cultural time demands have buried landmines we need to avoid. The *REST* criteria can help us joyfully relax with Christ and reinforce our resolve to glorify Him.

"R" means we want God to *remind* us of His past week's gifts. Gratitude follows. Note that we are the recipients postured in humility. If we presumptively generate the list, we are vulnerable to not noticing what God graciously gave. Asking the Lord to review and reveal the past six days with us allows us to begin in sheer wonder. Gratitude, as we've seen already, is highly correlated with joy. Note that we are making our gritty choice to ask the Lord to show us *ALL* of the good He's provided. Expect to be surprised! Celebrate His perfect timing, even when it's not fully known. Notice what He began to do in the last week that is more like a seed planted than fruit harvested. The more time we make available for this remembrance review, the more we'll cultivate the habit of thankful attentiveness.

"E" means to *enjoy* who you are and *Whose* you are. The gift of rest was first practiced by God on the seventh day after He completed the work of creation. Adam's first agenda was to enjoy a full day of rest with God. Resting with God *for the next week's work* may be helpfully disruptive to those who mistakenly imagine that Sabbath's purpose is primarily to *rest from last week's work*. By the way, God does not need rest:

> Have you never heard? Have you never understood? The LORD is the everlasting God, the Creator of all the earth. He never grows weak or weary. No one can measure the depths of his understanding.[193]

Why did God rest? Having made all of His creation, He declared it was *very good,* blessed this final day, and made it holy. We the created *do* have a physical need for rest, but recuperation is at best secondary to enjoying God's loving companionship. The American god of utility can't be allowed to intrude on this purpose.[194] When our efforts have the singular focus of leading us into a trusting relationship with Jesus, we all discover what history knows: He always comes through. So much more than a refreshing pause, *REST* provides space to be transformed.[195]

Enjoying who we are leads us to contemplate our privileged status as God's beloved. Jesus asserted that His kingdom is reserved for the childlike.[196] If severe and sober reflection excludes playfulness, we wonder if we're missing something important in Jesus' heart. Describing adults who are "imprisoned by self-consciousness," Rick Lawrence commended the "scandal of childlikeness" for how we can live in the spirit of God's "deep delight."[197]

Once Eb and I became acquainted with the interplay between knowing Jesus and discovering how He sees us, it seemed like the pages of Scripture—especially the Gospels—explode with evidence of this sequencing. It's a natural next step to carve out time to be with spouses, children, friends, etc. The Lord delights in them and He invites us to join His fondness for them. In shared worship, we savor God's presence, gaze appreciatively on all He has done, and celebrate. Our gritty identity is reinforced. Jesus "ruins" us by consuming us. And, joyfully, we pay close attention to what God pronounces over us: It is *all very good*.

"S" means we *stop* doing what makes us restless. If it feels like work, don't do it. This will require honest soul searching about what makes us restless. Social media proves that not all leisure deserves that label. News reports are seldom restful, even if we watched them while blanketed on the couch. If it induces restlessness, it does not pass the *REST* criteria. We *strongly* recommend to all of us *nomophobics* and FOMO addicts (see chapter 4) that some version of turning off the phone is warranted. Eb and I have seen how collecting these pocket interrupters from teens before a retreat experience or weeklong camp—something initially met with protests—is an offering of availability to God's Spirit that proves fruitful. But this habit is not one-size-fits-all. What is restful to one person may be work to another.

If someone's labor is mostly computer-oriented, mowing the lawn can be a restful conversational exercise with God. On the other hand, as a rabid Cubs fan watching my team play in the World Series, I realized that my twisted stomach was anything but restful. I decided to turn off the TV on that Sunday, choosing to be more fully relaxed than I could be as a lifelong fan. We've got to notice restlessness within if we want to disrupt the pace for true joy with God. This is part of our attentiveness training.

That's how we counseled Jon, an urban youth minister and one of our cohort mentors from Columbus, Ohio. His teens had a practical question: *Could they play basketball on Sunday?* Our answer was that they should play then talk about whether the game was restful to their hearts or stressful to their souls. Not everyone is at their best when playing hoops. That's why we need *GUEST* partners who keep it real and can help us notice what we might not see. In Indy's "Purpose Park," (see chapter 1) 15-year-old Dustin called out his leader, Danny, for being angry while playing ball. To his credit, Danny owned it. Then he gently reminded his young friend that he had asked everyone's forgiveness for his behavior.

There's one more dimension to consider for work stoppage. *Avoid doing what's necessary.* This takes planning, but it's worth it. When we let necessity creep into our day of rest with God, we give obligation a foothold. It's better to think about "wasting time" with God than doing something that needs to be done.

"T" means to *take* hope with God into your next week. We often gain joy by anticipating that something long-awaited will actually happen or work we care about will finally be completed. Surrendering these highly invested dreams to the Lord is both an act of worship and an expression of trust. What do you think the young man who gave up his two fish and five loaves felt at the moment he handed them to Jesus' disciple? How much joy do you think he experienced when the entire throng was fed by his contribution? One of the features of *REST* as a habit is that we will weekly have the opportunity to put the days ahead and work to be done into God's hands. Let there be prayers of consecration over every calendar entry as we plan. This is an element of preparedness that can be renewed weekly. It is fortified by a growth mindset and feeds grit's desire to push forward and gain ground on our most cherished goal.

The habit of *REST* is the most unfamiliar takeaway from our multi-year discovery process. Frankly, making this concept practical has been the biggest challenge of all. Our testimony is not that we've locked it down, but that growing grit with Jesus is compelling us to work it out. If excuses kill off our efforts, we don't demonstrate anything close to grit. At least that's why Eb and I tackled *REST*—and it keeps us messing around in our own life labs. Our *GUEST* partnerships also keep us going. The *INVEST* and *TEST* habits, which we explain in the following chapters, feed into *REST*, but *REST* also makes stunning contributions to all of the other habits. We think it's sensible for us to be able to push a weekly reset button that serves our all-consuming love relationship with God. Anything is possible when days without urgency are protected each week. We're growing more durable joy by practicing an ancient habit we've ignored for most of our lives.

We also have a gnawing sensation that this habit can be a trap. It sure was for the religious leaders in Jesus' day. Our safeguard is tucked into the clarity of our gritty focus. And we've been powerfully moved by those whose grit helps us understand what we aspire to. Brother Lawrence is such a trailblazer. His determination to know Jesus led him away from small-minded confinement to see how *IT'S ALL GOOD.*

Brother Lawrence was a seventeenth-century monk assigned to serve his Paris monastery as a dishwasher. While scrubbing pots and pans, he sought to continuously *practice the presence of God*. It's because of the book by that title that we know him today. (We giggle to realize that his grit might have given him Brillo-pad efficiency in his dutiful cleaning.) His clear passion was to become so deeply and enjoyably aware of God's constant presence that he insisted on forming a habit of continual conversation with Him no matter what else is going on in the day. Further, this practice would eventually yield the inward and inextinguishable joy from being God's beloved.[198]

Like Paul who pressed on to learn what he needed,[199] every setback was a growth opportunity for Lawrence, who cautioned against discouragement if we fail in early efforts. As we persist in our practices, we can expect an intentional discipline to grow into a delightful and natural habit.[200]

Brother Lawrence practiced what we've labeled a "Failure Strategy" and it's a tremendous encouragement to all of us otherwise discouraged by our erratic faithfulness. Self-examination, especially during the routines of mundane work, invites the Lord to express pleasure in how we've done our duty or reveals the need for asking forgiveness. Both are cherished gifts for those who share Brother Lawrence's ultimate passion to grow in grace and love for God.[201] There is no need to be anxious about failing if we are humble and hungry to learn. This is how we are drawn into the joyful companionship of Christ and welcome the gentle tutoring He offers.[202] There is in-the-moment benefit to be gained whenever we've got a mind to grow.

Brother Lawrence rejected the notion that there could be anything in life that does not pertain to God. With this conviction, he sought to always give attention to God's presence and then cling to Him. He trained himself to leverage every moment as an opportunity to surrender control, yielding the joy of loving obedience so simple and outlandishly practical that this attentiveness should suffice as any preacher's focus.[203] His efforts to grow followed patterns of experimentation and reflection. For example, he once reported how he had resolved to make loving God the ultimate purpose of every activity, engaging in the smallest chore or work assignment for no other reason.[204] So certain was he that he could enjoy God's presence anywhere and anytime, that he refused to consider what's commonly understood as religious activity to be more pleasing to the Lord than ordinary work or even mundane work.[205]

The experience of Christ's companionship was continual, it was disruptive, and it ushered Brother Lawrence into joy.[206] He had no naiveté about the persistent efforts it would take to cultivate this ongoing communication with God. It's in that sense that Brother Lawrence represents how we believe grit research can be applied to our relationship with God. Far from being passive about time, he disrupted its pace, obsessively intent on doing his work well by trusting the companionship of our good and loving God.[207]

Here is an exemplar who seemed able to hold together the challenge of living a life full of three constants: joy, prayer, and gratitude.[208] Becoming Lawrence-like in our own grit with Jesus is the essence of the disruption challenge we want to offer parents and youth ministers. To delight in relating with God and others unleashes our brain's joy to engage the world—even in solitary experience—as the best versions of ourselves.[209]

Adults who want to point teens to prevailing joy with Jesus have plenty of daily-grind experiences like dishwashing. Brother Lawrence's genius was flipping mundane moments into faith-stretching opportunities. Gritty faith gets clarified when we test it against both adversity *and* normalcy.

I once sent some adults I was teaching on a five-minute walkabout, inviting them to roam the halls of our church and look for things that annoyed them. When they came back together, it was clear that the assignment was too easy! Their critiques picked up steam as their griping grew. I quickly called a timeout and dispatched them on another five-minute challenge: "Notice something in the building that gives you reason to be thankful to the Lord." This, too, proved easy. But their responses were a bit less chatty as they realized with some chagrin the point of this lesson. God's gifts are everywhere; it's not hard to name them.

145

So why don't we enjoy God's grace more than we do? We think it's because gratitude grows when we give it space to grow. *And we're too busy to do so!*

What's true for us applies exponentially to teens. If we're going to soak in God's grace, we need to disrupt our pace. *REST* can help us become attentive to Jesus. God is not difficult to locate, nor are His gifts in scarce supply. In fact, it's just the opposite. We're like insatiable sponges. If our soaking saturates us and we could constantly return for more after being squeezed out, we will never exhaust the limits of God's grace. But it seems we prefer quick rinse-offs in God's showers of blessing to luxuriant bubble baths. There's something messed up in us that needs to be disrupted. We've succumbed to a life-pace that robs us of soul-marinating joy.

The super-power Brother Lawrence cultivated was becoming constantly attentive to Jesus. He's worth emulating. And we've realized that the genius of *REST* as a weekly day set aside with God is that it cultivates this same quality. Brother Lawrence was a *noticer*. We've gotten better at noticing throughout the week because it's a feature of our *REST* habit practice. It makes sense that we who aren't yet able to see as well as Lawrence could benefit from enrolling in God's original introductory class of Sabbath-keeping.

Could our adult practice of *REST* be a difference-maker among the teens we love?

Throughout this book, we've used a diving metaphor to explain how the life we aspire to is one that is *retrieved from the depths with Jesus.* Brother Lawrence is a historical exemplar, showing us where to invest passionate persistence. Grit-growing necessitates habits that can develop the "different muscle groups"[210] needed to dive with Jesus. Much like we might hear from a personal trainer's coaching plan for our physical muscles, these spiritual muscles should be tailored to strengthen different target areas. Like gym workouts, our efforts are intended to be *disruptive.* Brother Lawrence's best practices inspire us to pursue *constant Sabbath rest* that goes beyond the law's expectations, just as Jesus modeled and taught. We need directional habits that are weighty. This one helps us become more Jesus-attentive.

For now, it's important to understand how the identity-grounded good life that adolescents desperately need to see modeled is *only found in the depths with Jesus.* David Kinnaman and Mark Matlock reach a similar, research-based conclusion, and we join them in decrying how youth ministry falls short: "The church has responded to the identity pressures of our culture by offering young people a Jesus 'brand experience' rather than facilitating a transformational experience to find their identity in the person and work of Jesus."[211]

Disrupting the less-than-fruitful pace of our lives, Jesus' timely whispers of soul-targeted truth transform who we are. The boys in Eldora lockup share a kindred desire with Brother Lawrence: to discover how joy retrieved with Jesus in our soul's deep waters is portable. Once young people discover who Jesus is, how to enjoy Him, how He enjoys them, and who they are, the upward journey will excite them as they anticipate—well—*anything.*

CAUTION

*Habits can be useful because
our brains ache for efficiency.
But this efficiency lies beneath the
awareness we need to choose love.*

In customizing my *REST* habit, I've even penned the occasional poem. As those who pay for their children's liberal arts education have observed, poetry hardly seems *useful.* It's the language of lovers, a great way to waste time in rapt attentiveness with the Lord.

To our way of thinking, that makes poetry a *REST* day experience worth attempting.

Disrupt the Pace
by Dave Rahn

I want to exceed this cursed speed, if I can.
Be freed from the orbit so common to man.
Contriving, then driving,
I long to be thriving —
But my heart is a seed in need of God's scan.

There's a lingering stink in each blink of my pride.
I think to impress with how hard I have tried.
Deflecting...detecting...
Some impulse reflecting
Arouses my heart—Can I be taught how to glide?

To soar high in God's breeze on my knees without
flapping.
Join the trees and creation in gratitude clapping.
Jesus shook free of death's dust,
Cracked my crust, gained my trust.
Rise to please Him, O heart—Awake from your napping!

Leap to listen, not race; it's grace I crave most.
My pace hinders hearing: *"Beloved...come close!"*
Now let grit's custom fit
Steer my steed—like a bit—
Into joy, and the space where rest's Tutor is host.

Grace, avail in my story!
Christ's gifts stir my wonder.
Joy, prevail in my story!
Love's strikes prompt my thunder.
For glory—His glory—my story! Amen.

Endless obligations crush us. Young people see little evidence that our faith is fixing our *do-more* disease. At their identity core is a mess of flailing activity. They can neither rejoice always nor be thankful for everything because Jesus has yet to disrupt their pace.

Can Jesus really provide *REST* with Him, no matter how much we all have to do? In addition to the one amateur poem offered, consider this iconic line from Shakespeare's Hamlet: "To be, or not to be: That is the question:" (3.1.1749).[212]

Let's be clear. The habit of *REST* dedicates a day each week to becoming more Jesus-attentive than we are. It's a heart-triggering opportunity, nothing more. If postured in humility, we open ourselves to the flow of God's grace, grow our grit, and experience joy with Jesus.

Joyful Disruptions

Q1. What are you grateful for from the last week?

Q2. What makes you restless?

Q3. What do you think makes our teens restless?

Q3. How can God grow more of your trust by resting with Him?

CHAPTER 11

INVEST: Jesus-Responsive

Amy Binkley is one of those gifted people who could build a significant relational connection with a telephone pole. Quickly. She's just that good with people. And she's fearless. Overcoming her suburban mom status (she has two adult children) was only a slight learning curve for her when she agreed to join the ministry leadership team investing in Youth for Christ City Life girls. She's learned plenty about urban life and has enjoyed flaunting her street patois around me. Relentlessly authentic and doggedly intent, Amy consistently shows up in teenagers' lives to serve and share Christ. Importantly, she has no tolerance for ministry tactics that aren't practical.

When we looked for local leaders who could host a few older adolescents in an eight-week habit-training adventure, Amy didn't hesitate to volunteer. Enthusiastically, she did her best to follow guidelines for the small group we asked her to lead that summer.

Amy spent the gift card we sent her to buy *Find Joy in the Journey* t-shirts for her ladies. Ashley and Lydia did not know each other at all prior to Amy inviting them into her small group. By the conclusion of their eight weeks together, they had forged a pretty deep three-person connection. Soon Ashley and Lydia built on their new bond to co-lead a group with younger inner-city girls.

Amy is confident that their shared outreach is due to the deep trust they formed while learning how to experience more joy, more often by companion living with Jesus. She began overseeing Ashley and Lydia, watching His joy spill over onto their group's high school girls. She was excited to trace how far the relational ripple would travel from its origin in an eight-week "joy with Jesus" social experiment one summer.

We all need models to help us walk in constant, joyful companionship with the Lord. Where do we look when, as Eb's kids Caleb and Lily hinted during spaghetti dinner (see chapter 5), inspiring examples aren't readily seen in our everyday world? Grit's dogged determination leads us to treasure every crumb that someone has left to follow the trail we want to travel.

Eb and I now see how our back stories parallel Paul's in Philippians 3. Lots of prior efforts in this faith journey were misdirected until, by God's grace, we agree that "everything else is worthless when compared with the infinite value of knowing Christ Jesus my Lord. For his sake I have discarded everything else, counting it all as garbage, so that I could gain Christ and become one with him."[213] We've been drawn to the research about grit because we think it can launch us into the deep places we want to go. Like Paul, we make no claim about "having arrived," but we share his willingness to declare that there will be no turning back from this direction.[214]

Paul wrapped up his powerful testimony-to-confession in Philippians with these words: "Let all who are spiritually mature agree on these things. If you disagree on some point, I believe God will make it plain to you. But we must hold on to the progress we have already made."[215] We share his assertion that pressing on to know Christ is the only end goal worth pursuing, and we're jumping onboard with enthusiasm and conviction. For this clearly focused, whatever-it-takes grit, Paul set an example.[216]

You see where this is taking us, right? All of us need models; our kids may be the most desperate of all. Where will we point them?

At this point a few years ago, Eb and I could be heard saying (or rather, praying) *"O, wow—how are we going to become examples?!"* Well-aimed habits like we're commending had not been part of our early days of being formed in youth ministry. If we're going to be of help to young people and their families, we knew greater change was needed. So, in choosing joy with Jesus, we've signed on to welcome disruption.

With practical Amy hovering in our minds, we are doing some things to make this journey work, wary to avoid settling for less than the gritty passion Paul described. In Chapter 9 we identified the discipline of meeting weekly with trusted *GUEST* partners to become more Jesus-connected. Then we looked at the habit of setting aside a day each week for *REST* that helps us become more Jesus-attentive. Now we want to advocate for an effort to seek, hear from, and respond to what Jesus wants from us for that day.

INVEST is a daily routine of uninterrupted dialogue with the risen Christ. Both of us agree that this is when Jesus does His deepest work in our lives. By settling into quiet space reserved for careful listening, we learn to recognize His voice. Giving Him the early portion of our day, before our minds hustle off to the work ahead, helps us cultivate tutor-friendly ears. Jesus promises to teach willing listeners.[217] We prove our hunger to hear by how we *INVEST* the first, fresh moments after we awaken.

Hearing and recognizing Jesus' voice is the listening condition that separates His sheep from all others.[218] When He taught something that was hard to understand or difficult to accept, would-be students either bought in or they didn't. Those are the only two response categories available. Parables were shaped to make sense exclusively for followers awaiting a word from God to act on.[219] Whether we obey what we hear Jesus teach distinguishes the faithful from the foolish.[220] Old Testament leaders like Abraham, Moses, and David fall under the first heading. Other nations, Pharaoh, King Saul, and Judah's remnant during the Babylonian exile[221] fail this wisdom test. Christ's letters to seven churches are custom coaching directives with varying degrees of encouragement and rebuke. But all end on the same note, warning readers in exactly the same way: "Anyone with ears to hear must listen to the Spirit and understand what he is saying to the churches."[222]

The writer of Hebrews draws upon a song of David[223] to label this affliction *hardheartedness*, a disqualifying condition when it comes to enjoying God's restful companionship.[224] Significantly, this passage is punctuated by back-to-back statements crucial to understanding the dynamics at work in practicing our *INVEST* habit:

For the word of God is alive and powerful. It is sharper than the sharpest two-edged sword, cutting between soul and spirit, between joint and marrow. It exposes our innermost thoughts and desires. Nothing in all creation is hidden from God. Everything is naked and exposed before his eyes, and he is the one to whom we are accountable. So then, since we have a great High Priest who has entered heaven, Jesus the Son of God, let us hold firmly to what we believe. This High Priest of ours understands our weaknesses, for he faced all of the same testings we do, yet he did not sin. So let us come boldly to the throne of our gracious God. There we will receive his mercy, and we will find grace to help us when we need it most.[225]

The *INVEST* habit prioritizes time each day to engage Scripture and become more Jesus-responsive than we are. Our "innermost thoughts and desires" are part of this engagement. Nothing is to be off-limits or hidden from view in this very personal time with the Lord. Profoundly, Jesus relates to us simultaneously as the ultimately supreme Lord of creation and someone who "gets us." His love for us is not only limitless, it's targeted to flow into the areas of our lives where help is most needed. Amazing grace, always at work. Why would we not rush our positive RSVP to His invitation to meet with Him personally? Daily? Deeply?

Perhaps, to put it gently, a preference for control over disruption exposes our hard-heartedness. Sin's wreckage is personally devastating. It masks how pride and fear can still roam our hearts. Our too-common default posture is not the bent knee of humility. It's the assertive stance of refusal. We do what we do because that's what we do.

When we *INVEST* priority time to listen, learn, and act quickly to obey Jesus—to become *Jesus-responsive*—we unleash gritty resolve for the sake of knowing Him and retrieving joy with Him. The published *State of the Bible 2024* by American Bible Society points to a downward trend in any kind of Bible use by adults since 2021; only 38% fell into this category in 2024.[226] The *INVEST* habit reflects serious intent that will place us among top-end outliers among Bible users. Churches are not unaware of the transformational power tucked inside this habit. In data collected from hundreds of thousands of congregants, involving more than 1,000 churches between September 2008 and March

2010,[227] researchers concluded that daily Scripture engagement is the single greatest predictor of spiritual vitality.[228]

Our thoughts are the subatomic elements in our formation. Without training, they fly into our minds from all directions. We live—too often—as randomized Christians. But if we can establish this *INVEST* habit, we will submit to the mental makeover so crucially linked to trusting God, rejoicing always, and being constantly appreciative.[229] Since grateful teens are an endangered species with a bent toward random living, this is an ambitious goal. The way grit works is that where there's a will there's a way. We intentionally meet with Jesus in a listen-learn-obey posture daily, giving Bible engagement our full concentration and best effort, assessing whether what we did delivered what we seek. Then we keep repeating—tweaking—innovating—improving. Our *INVEST* habit gets continual refinement efforts because the stakes are so high.[230] We'll borrow from Brother Lawrence's "Failure Strategy" (see chapter 10) in order to love the Lord with all our hearts, souls, minds, and strength. This is one way grit disrupts our pace for an uncommon passion.

When we trained the young people in our research to engage the Bible, we explained that reading a passage needed a "plus one" experience. Engaging is deep-dive worthy; simply reading too easily devolves into surface check-listing. Electronic media's deluge has trained teens to skim quickly. To counter this, we asked participants to choose at least one of six options beyond a daily reading: 1) meditate on it, 2) pray over it, 3) talk about it, 4) memorize part of it, 5) write about it, or 6) act on it. Each of these qualify as engagement strategies that help us become more *Jesus-responsive* than we currently are.

There are 150 psalms in Scripture. David wrote at least half of them. Some reflect the tranquil meditation enjoyed by a shepherd boy. Others are a warrior's desperate plea for rescue and protection from enemies. Seven have been labeled *penitential psalms*; these were written after King David abused his power to commit adultery and then orchestrate a murder to cover up his sin. David's venerated status in the grand plans of God—in spite of his tragic failures—leads us to conclude that a man or woman "after God's own heart"[231] is identified by responsive obedience to God's frequently disruptive Word.

Picture how a small band of jazz musicians improvises in performance.[232] They respond on time to one another. "When we understand more intimately what motivates [Jesus], we can relax and enter into our relationship with him in a more adventurous way." Rick Lawrence described how in a "Drumline Relationship" 1) instinct draws us to 2) respond to Jesus' lead 3) fearlessly 4) from our heart's authentic depth.[233]

Our habits are forces to be reckoned with in becoming responsive. *INVEST* is probably my most established habit, so much so, that when I bolted out of bed with a thoughtful conviction (slow brain) that I should immediately act to finish outdoor yard work begun yesterday, I did so with my *INVEST* habit nipping at my heels. I returned to my coffee, Scripture, and unhurried listening posture two hours later, a bit weary for the gritty exertion I used to consciously respond to Jesus, *seeming* to ignore my deeply cherished habit. My nagging brain's white-sheathed super-highway neural-system needed to be reminded that *JESUS IS LORD*. The joy that followed reminded me of playground triumphs that ended with "Nah-nah-nah-nah-nah-nah!"

On June 17, 2024, an opinion page guest essay was published by the *New York Times*. Its author was Dr. Vivek Murthy, United States Surgeon General, and its purpose was to call for a warning label on social media platforms because there is an emergency mental health crisis among young people and their social media use is an important contributor. Adolescents spending three or more hours daily in online social media are twice as vulnerable to depression and anxiety—and their average time spent during the summer of 2023 was 4.8 hours.[234] The evidence deserves *at least* this call to action from all of us who love young people.

Young people desperately need caring adults who show them how to disrupt soul-crushing lies with love-birthed truth. When music captures this angst *and* offers psalm-like authenticity, it's a grit asset. A sequence of five songs from singer/songwriter Lauren Daigle and collaborators sits atop my playlist to remind me how God's heart for me is the deepest truth of all, no matter how broken I feel: *Love Like This, First, Trust in You, You Say,* and *Look Up Child.*[235]

To *INVEST* is to prioritize beliefs that renew our minds through the daily habit rigor. As is his responsibility, the Surgeon General urged adults to act immediately so our young people are protected. But the enemy's intent to steal, kill, and destroy is beyond his scope, and doesn't need technology to be accomplished. Our vigilance must exceed societal measures to do no harm. Let's retrieve from Jesus' deep heart the abundant life He offers.[236] We can't lead young people into this joy if we don't know the way. *INVEST* can help.

CAUTION

*Habits can be useful because
our brains ache for efficiency.
But this efficiency lies beneath the
awareness we need to choose love.*

When routines make our efforts mechanical, they're doing what our brain wants from them. To act like something is second nature conserves energy. Have you ever been tempted to approach morning devotional time as a checklist item? We have. In the fellowship of the sheepish, we might further confess the pride we feel by never missing a day. Better to skip on occasion so as to guard our hearts from such Pharisaism.

If this were rocket science, it might be hard to remain humble. Catching ourselves distracted in someone's company, we simply refocus. Listening to what they're saying and responding lovingly shows basic respect. Why not give at least this sort of effort to God? Once a day. Early is better, before other priorities clamor for our attention is best.

The gritty innovate to chase their passion. Way too many of us—adults who *lead* young people—practice *INVEST* habits that have degraded over time. At one time they were invigorating: now they're anemic. That's where I found myself a few years ago. In search of something that worked, I tried something new. Since listening to Jesus has been the insistent centerpiece of my pursuit, that's my intent in Scripture engagement too. I pull passages from four different sections of the Bible each day. Poised with my journal, I jot down threads that connect these different passages. Each time I see similarities, I notice that my own curiosity is aroused. This is intriguing to me. I perk up, asking God whether this is what He wants me to know or understand or act upon that day. I'm not studying to prep a lesson for someone else—I'm gathering manna for the day. The reading primes my focus, draws me into conversation. And the "four passage strategy" helps me avoid the trap of only traveling in my most favorite and familiar Bible terrain. *INVEST* has become my pacemaker, jolting me into intimacy with Jesus.

Wanting to hear from Jesus first and foremost is a desire that, ultimately, we can't self-generate. It's a salvation extension, a gift of grace that squashes all boasting under our joyful expressions of uninhibited gratitude.[237]

Let's be clear. This habit will *INVEST* priority time each day engaging Scripture to become more Jesus-responsive than we are. It's a heart-triggering opportunity and it must not be confused with earnest Bible study that hosts an additional benefit without the brain's habit-forming structure. If postured in humility, we open ourselves to the flow of God's grace, grow our grit, and experience joy with Jesus.

Joyful Disruptions

Q1. How often do you engage Scripture to hear from Jesus? What does it look like?

Q2. What could you try to make Scripture engagement more life-giving?

Q3. If you knew Jesus wanted you to do something, why might you hesitate?

Q4. How can adults better inspire teens to engage Scripture?

CHAPTER 12

TEST: JESUS-AUTHENTIC

Habit-forming, as it turns out, takes dedicated effort. Whatever else might be said of Brother Lawrence, it was his relentless passion to experience Christ's presence in every moment that led him to form habits that worked. Research suggests it's worth it to grow such habits. These are efforts that need to work, especially when things get tough.

Adversity exposes the strength of our relationship with Jesus. Do we experience Jesus coming through in real-time, when our needs are most urgent? It's this too-common reality among urban young people, especially, that motivated us to look for *prevailing* joy. Far from being a predictor of weak faith, we suspect the presence of adversity is the white-hot furnace that God uses to forge gritty followers of Christ.

Ebonie's sick husband became such a person in her life. He challenged her to find new resolve at the depths of who she was, where Jesus wanted to tutor her. Clay's urgent need for a liver transplant heightened Eb's sense this was an insistent journey.

Her activities in church continued, but her attention shifted to Jesus. There was always something to be grateful for. The couple's fertility struggles were another crushing burden— and then Eb conceived, birthing a son the same year Clay was supposed to die. In fact, the countdown clock ticking in Ebonie's head about Clay's life expectancy faded as three years grew to five and—still counting! Ebonie met Jesus routinely and deeply as she engaged Scripture. This opened her heart to hear what others had been telling her: God was calling Eb into ministry.

Jesus' companionship was tangible. It's a fact that ministry traffics in adversity. But Jesus-responsiveness kept fortifying Eb's new understanding of herself. Her sister's drug-related murder meant she and Clay would become parents to two broken children. The younger became a daughter; the older introduced heartache by dissolving back into the world. Dad died. Eb's brother let a drug habit spin out of control and, for a while, Eb and Clay fostered then prepared to adopt a nephew. An anguishing decision after two years prevented that from taking place. That's the week I invited her into my discovery journey about Sabbath rest and joy.

Perfect timing, right? In Psalm 42:7, David observed that "deep calls to deep." Reflecting on this, Spurgeon said our pain's depth exposes the depth of God's love:

> Open now your ears and your hearts, to hear the calling of this deep unto its brother deep. Hearken while I translate the echoes of truth. Inasmuch as you have many trials, remember the depth of the divine faithfulness. You have not been able to comprehend the reason of your trials, but I beseech you believe in the firmness and stability of the divine affection toward you. In proportion to your tribulations shall be your consolations. If you have shallow sorrows, you shall receive but shallow graces; but if you have deep afflictions, you shall obtain the deeper proofs of the faithfulness of God ... Great deeps of trial bring with them great deeps of promise.[238]

Here's Eb's summary: "*I found Jesus in the deep. He coaxes me and coaches me to strengthen my heart. Jesus' faithfulness is unmatched, the joy He offers unspeakable. Even to me.*" This is why I asked Eb to join my research-writing adventure. But I had NO idea about her horrific backstory until a month before our writing was done. We blame Rick Lawrence who has described himself as "ruined by Jesus." Such friends aren't hesitant to spread the ruination.

It happened when Rick plunked down across from Ebonie at the event where I introduced Frank Bell to youth ministry educators. We were on a riverboat dinner cruise, and I could see them engaged in conversation. Rick is thoughtful, curious, and fearless—a seasoned journalist. Before long, Eb shared what you have read, but I didn't then know. He pressed Eb to describe her joy in light of all she's been through. With more conviction than eloquence Eb stated what we've since adopted as our relationship banner during our companion diving: "*I don't know. Just Jesus. That's it. Jesus.*"

Sometimes when we say something that's strange (even to us), we walk away and imagine what we *should* have said. After replaying her answer hundreds of times, Eb has dug in. Her joy comes from being with Jesus. It's now crystal clear to her that Jesus is redeeming every hard experience she has endured. Like me, she's more of a habit novice than an expert. But we've become acquainted with how grit with Jesus works, met people who've made it work, and know we can't turn back. There's plenty yet to discover.

Ebonie's husband, Clay, remains on the roster for liver transplants. His current medical challenges have intensified. Sometimes adversity is a catastrophic event, like the death of a family member. It can also be chronic, bringing a weird "normalcy" to things like alcohol abuse in the home. When we see an accident coming our way, we brace for impact, triggering adrenaline to surge into "overcoming overdrive." When adversity is more like erosion, it dangerously covers-up its incremental destruction. Mere pests don't trigger us to be heroes. But unless our joy with Jesus also conquers mundane normalcy and general complacency, it can't be confirmed as "prevailing."

The really good news is that our response to any challenge, great or small, can be exactly the same, as Ebonie testifies. Tragic events, boring jobs, snarled traffic, tenuous health, severe mercies—whatever it is, Jesus' companionship is enough for us to rejoice always. "God might sooner cease to be than cease to be faithful," wrote Spurgeon.[239] Our grit is locked in. The Great Disruptor extends love so that Ebonie's ACE scores (see chapter 4) don't matter. *Jesus. Just Jesus.*

Louis Chaney has worked with middle schoolers in Greensboro for 32 years. A certified lifeguard, his love for water led him to snorkel in some pretty exotic places. But after becoming open water certified for scuba diving, he embraced a new favorite sport. "There's no comparison," he gushes when asked what makes scuba so much better than snorkeling. Why? For starters, the whole "borrowed air" experience fascinates him. "You have to learn how to relax. Some can't handle this; they hyperventilate. I love getting in touch with the rhythm of my breathing patterns. It's all you can hear down below."

Poking around submerged cars and motorcycles at the bottom of a local quarry is one of his recurring adventures. But Louis can't get to the deep and explore *anything* without being all-in, physically and mentally. For him, scuba diving requires a complete disengagement from everything else. It's a rejuvenating disconnection, a space-maker.[240] Hearing this youth ministry veteran enthuse about a new favorite hobby reignites our prayers for this book. It's not too late to learn how to dive, rest, and enjoy discovery adventures with Jesus.

We have been pulled to explore how Jesus grows us from the inside-out through frequent and varied pace disruptions. In pursuit of integrity, our thoughts about disrupting the pace have been scattershot with fits, starts, stops, distractions, and countless interruptions. Please picture us with slow smiles growing, heads nodding in appreciation of God's skillful soul surgery. He is teaching us about loving disruptions through His loving disruptions. To recognize His hand at work in an otherwise annoying moment is to instantly move from darkness to light. Joy surges in bursts through our hearts. Our brains make swift calculations that are nonsensical unless we've learned relationship math: this moment is *God's gift for us!*

Counselors have become acquainted with a form of psychotherapy known as Eye Movement Desensitization and Reprocessing (EMDR). It aims to help people whose brains have been malformed by past trauma and chronic adversity. How? Disruption! It restructures existing neural networks. Elizabeth Miranda compared the brain to Jenga-like highways that forcefully direct our thoughts. EMDR works to deconstruct the old patterns and open up new pathways. "We can see brain mapping pictures that show the change," she said as she leaned in, "it's like I have a window into how God transforms people by renewing their minds!"[241] All truth is God's truth, and this research illuminates how God built our brains to work through hardwired systems that can be rewired. Reframing life experiences is a form of *renewing the mind!*

We were all created for disruptive, durable joy with Jesus. Adolescents might have a developmental advantage over adults in their joy journey. Except for the infant-toddler life stage, brain growth is greatest during adolescence. We need deep-diving insights of young people as much as they need ours.

My trek with Eb began in our shared here and now. Maybe it's more accurate to say, "Here and not quite yet." We imagined an empirical research pathway of discoveries whereby volunteers would agree to do what we asked over eight weeks. Then they would report whether it helped them gain steadier companionship and prevailing joy with Jesus. Enough strange setbacks to this plan eventually caught our attention. "What are we missing?" we asked.

This is a brave question. It ushered in our first major disruptive shift, pulling us first and foremost to notice the nuanced activity of God in our own hearts. We compared notes and eventually realized that in our *GUEST* partnership Eb and I acquired the relational brain-energy for problem-solving. Our stories continued to be informed by the personal quiet work God did through our individual *INVEST* practice habits. He met us privately, in deep, seldom-visited, places. These early morning visitations are usually co-sponsored by coffee (Dave) or crushed ice (Eb—don't try to figure it out). Between the two of us, we could see some of the same patterns in *how* He was teaching us, even as we sought to be faithful to *what* He wanted from us individually.

The trial-and-error-and-learn-and-improve adventure with regard to *REST* was the official reason for our inquiry. We noticed how quickly Sabbath practices could slide into burdensome duty and, in true gritty fashion, resolved to be exceptionally vigilant about keeping joyful rest with God as our focus. This ultimately led us to be careful not to romanticize Sabbath-keeping. Its formal practices can become more important than the relationship alignment it's intended to provide. Nobody wants a legalistic date night.

You may have noticed that, though we've spent more than half a century in the youth ministry world, we don't obsess over that focus. Call it collateral damage. Stories about how to get teens laughing so hard they pee themselves now bore us. Youth ministry has settled comfortably—and dangerously— into splash and snorkel activity. Parents have supported this. We coach kids with illustrations we've spent hours working on. We design killer retreats, hoping teens will be wowed enough to invite their friends. We swap creative ideas for social interaction, or hot learning discussions, or buzz-worthy fun. This use of time testifies to who we are, not just to what we can do.

Too many adults bring their own impoverished identities into the mix with young people. No wonder teens are baffled when they match Paul's words to their own faith experiences: "And now, just as you accepted Christ Jesus as your Lord, you must continue to follow him. Let your roots grow down into him, and let your lives be built on him. Then your faith will grow strong in the truth you were taught, and you will overflow with thankfulness."[242] The context of Paul's admonition is as clear and simple as Ebonie's confession to Rick Lawrence on the Mississippi River in October 2018. He was pressing to give believers "complete confidence that they understand God's mysterious plan, which is Christ himself."[243] This is the glorious secret that the once-slave nation of Israel could not possibly imagine: that "Christ lives in you."[244] Our "real life is hidden with Christ in God."[245] When we know ourselves in this way, as Paul and Ebonie insist, we can plunge into deep waters with adolescents until they, too, retrieve the best version of themselves. Sabrina, my friend and former student, once described this as a "necessary gutting" of her identity by Jesus.[246]

Dangerously high scores on the ACEs scale aren't needed to conclude that mixed experiences of Jenga-brain construction have malformed most, if not all of us. The failure of God's shepherds is, at times, a tragic betrayal of their charge to protect, as Eb experienced when she was 13. And yet here she is standing, testifying, discovering daily how to live into her calling.[247] Our identity deep dives cannot begin too soon, and they must not be hurried. *Jesus—just Jesus*—can be trusted. This Jesus is grit's true north. He alone can deliver constantly grateful joy. May such companion diving supplant the "how-to" questions that fascinate snorkelers.

Habits are fueled by cravings.[248] Our relational identity is the most important focus of our brain's fast track system. When we experience the joy of right relationships—including the sense of being true to ourselves—it seems our behind-the-scenes control center smooths the way, regardless of the difficulties we may be facing.[249]

What drove Brother Lawrence to cultivate his habits? There was certainly nothing fancy about his approach; he was emphatic about the fact that entering God's presence required no special skill, training, or knowledge. Anyone with a heart fully committed to know and love God above anyone or anything can go to God.[250] Ebonie's conclusion resonates throughout history. Jesus, simply Jesus, is enough for those who get to know Him.

Impressed by their formational power, we hope to locate habits that help us deep-dive with Jesus for prevailing joy. Gritty faith works itself out through focused habits. They will be necessarily disruptive[251] to gain what we're most passionate about.

Fearlessly, we've resorted to rhyming each of the four habits we suggest for this journey: *GUEST, REST, INVEST*, and now, *TEST*.

(Blame me. Ebonie is far too cool to do this.) Habit acquisition requires time for our brains to establish a new super-highway. Remember that the brain's white matter insulation process takes at least a month to form before these habits will save us energy. After taking shape, they can each make very specific contributions to our deep-diving joy retrieval.

The fourth practice we suggest, *TEST*, requires very little skill. Located as we burst back onto the surface where everyone else is splashing around, *TEST* has a double meaning. First, it reflects the adversity proving ground that verifies when faith-as-grit is authentic. Then, it's a shorthand for how we "testify" about Jesus while we're going through those challenges. We seem to *always* be in proximity of some kind of difficulty.

By practicing *TEST*, we upgrade this adversity-testimony link and return to an immersive relationship with our *hesed* God. Satan pounces on the Lord's mysterious timing to stalk our hearts, enfeebling our grit. But God wants to crush every impulse to seize control until we trust Him completely. We know Him during painful waiting in very different ways than we do in exultant victory. Much deeper. As He wants us to. The enemy has permission to beat us to our essence because God has purpose in working His love into our core being.[252] We beloved who have been fruitful with Jesus will be pruned for greater fruit,[253] and every moment, day, or season of difficulty is shaped for a reason linked to our joyful fulfillment.[254]

When—not *if*—we are hammered by adversity, it's purposeful, like a blacksmith's finishing work. The fire, heat, and body blows are necessary. To search for words to express our trust on such days is fortified by a habit of resolve. We're graced with the right words when we open our mouth, however unpolished they may seem at the time. Sometimes the only thing that comes to mind is, "Jesus—just Jesus." Enough said.

This habit was a common identifier among first century followers of Christ. Many of them had only a few degrees of separation from one of the more than 500 people who saw Jesus alive after He was crucified.[255] Word-of-mouth from such witnesses made for a pretty amazing headline as these believers made Christ known "in Jerusalem, throughout Judea, in Samaria, and to the ends of the earth."[256]

The community in which I live is home to the third largest concentration of Amish in the country. When something newsworthy takes place, even without social media and 24-hour news reporting, it's remarkable how quickly the word gets out. If there's something to talk about the buzz is everywhere. *Anyone* knowing *someone* who has seen a once-dead man come to life has something to talk about.

Of course, the rest of their stories were pretty compelling, too. Early Christians spoke about Jesus from personal experience. My daughter and her husband once passed along what they learned firsthand from an Oscar-nominated composer about how he developed the songs for his musical. Now good friends with this artist and his wife, I like hearing stories of an entirely different nature from when they spend time together.

It's the same way with Jesus. The facts about Him are pretty fascinating. But when His story is the difference-making yeast in our own stories, we become much more than dutiful reporters, obligated to tell others a religious story. The Good News takes on the fresh excitement of *Breaking News*. We become infectious enthusiasts who can't stop talking about our experiences with Jesus.

In this way, when we speak about Him to others, the *TEST* habit is a natural extension of who we have become since He claimed the throne of our hearts. We're different enough from our old selves that people might notice and ask, "What's up?" That's the basis for Peter's coaching tip to other Christ-followers: "if someone asks about your hope as a believer, always be ready to explain it. But do this in a gentle and respectful way."[257]

The *TEST* task is simple enough. Openly speak the name of Jesus every day, revealing how He and you face current challenges together. In our habit-training cohorts around the country, we asked them to do so in natural conversations. We didn't think this was a terribly difficult assignment, but we were wrong. Ebonie asked her own teens, who we met earlier in chapter 5, to do a one-week test run of this habit. You can picture the dinner table debrief that mom led. Caleb felt awkward doing it with his peers and so only spoke Jesus' name once. Lily, who's a few years older, was a little more at ease with the challenge. She tackled it a few times, but then forgot about it. Both kids found it easier to mention Jesus' name with people they already knew were Christians.

Does "testimony awkwardness" diminish with age? That didn't appear to be true among our late-adolescent cohorts. For example, among the DC-area ladies that Eb led, personal and private faith expressions were almost always preferred over public witness.

But here's the thing. We weren't asking these young people to do anything except mention the name of Jesus in the midst of a normal conversation that also revealed life is hard. This isn't to be a *Blurt Jesus* bumper sticker or a thunderclap statement that's insensitive to what everyone is already talking about. It's to be a simple reference, revealing the active relationship we enjoy with Christ. If it's too hard to acknowledge that Jesus is part of our stories, we wonder if there's a gap in the depth of our experiences. As Christ taught, "What you say flows from what is in your heart."[258] What we say reveals what's important to us. Every. Single. Word.

Like every habit, we learn something valuable in the try-and-fail process. If it's too hard to mention Jesus' name in conversation without being boorish, this can become a great topic for the Lord's tutoring. Even if such simple testimony is difficult, articulation can illuminate reality[259] and increase believability.[260] Self-perception theory asserts that attitudes actually follow behaviors rather than cause them.[261] Weighing both Scripture and social science research, we're pretty stubborn about advocating for *TEST* as a habit. Whether fortifying our faith or representing Jesus, it can serve our gritty focus. We love how the simple act of injecting Jesus into a conversation will pull us into some degree of thoughtfulness and prayer lest we become obnoxious telemarketers. Notice how concern over "getting it wrong" can be a lovely pace disruption with Jesus.

The more natural (habitual) it is to talk openly about Jesus, the more we become aware of His companionship. This is not scripting teen testimonies. Just the opposite. We want to normalize our relationship with Christ such that the mention of His name is part of the unsurprising fabric of our lives, much like a married man might offhandedly talk about his wife.

Eb and I have been very intrigued by how naturally *TEST* shows up in our lives. After seeing this development, we concluded that every single habit contributes to our increased awareness of God's presence. He's active interiorly, squashing fears, nudging us to take risks, persistently peeling away veneer that masks who we are. We've observed how completely He surrounds us, revealing Himself in creation's dependability, our planned activities, and unexpected opportunities. Our most common failure is simply not *noticing* the Lord. As we speak aloud about what He's currently up to, we become more alert to what else He's doing. This habit has ridiculous frequency momentum. When *TEST* is a way of life, it becomes far more than a once-daily practice.

There's one more benefit to be had with this habit practice. Our ears perk up when we hear someone who, like us, wants Jesus to be known. This makes perfect sense. I've traveled through airports wearing my Cubs hat and engaged perfect strangers in some quick conversation about who should be pitching more out of the bullpen. Discovering and connecting with others who've already joined the journey is easy. We've named quite a few real-time companions: the Eldora ministry team, Danny Marquez, Ms. Jenny, Ms. Loretta, Frank Bell, Amy Binkley, Rick Lawrence, Don Talley, Roger, and David. Others have endured in our memories, like Charmaigne, Dave, and Troi. When we got acquainted with Brother Lawrence, we celebrated the "otherworldly" traveling companions with a host of available wisdom. Once in the historical past, now in Heaven, inspiring exemplars who share our grit with Jesus can help us do the deep dive into durable joy.

TESTIFY!
by Dave Rahn

Effort is empty unless grace is our ration
To disrupt the pace of misguided passion.
I'll fess up: I'm messed up
All dressed up in me.
Until Christ interrupts, "lost" is my fashion.

But with Jesus I learn I'm a masterpiece hung
Among allies who hear love's melodies sung.

I'll stack up: I'm jacked up
All backed up by Christ.
"*Faithfulness*" enough to splash joy on my tongue!

CAUTION

*Habits can be useful because
our brains ache for efficiency.
But this efficiency lies beneath the
awareness we need to choose love.*

Let's be clear. This *TEST* habit daily names Jesus to others, expressing that we trust Him in real-time challenges and becoming more Jesus-authentic than we are. It's a heart-triggering opportunity, nothing more. If postured in humility, we open ourselves to the flow of God's grace, grow our grit, and experience joy with Jesus.

Joyful Disruptions

Q1. When did you last mention the name of Jesus in a natural conversation?

Q2. Read Psalm 78:1–4. Who talks to your teens about the praiseworthy deeds of the Lord?

Q3. How does talking about Jesus amidst adversity reveal your faith is authentic?

Q4. How can parents and youth pastors partner to take teens deeper than the splash and snorkel zone?

EXHALE

GRITTY INHABITATION

True grit bears passion fruit. Michael Phelps climbed atop swimming world medal platforms because he spent countless hours of dedicated practice in the pool. When our utmost desire is to know Christ and walk joyfully with Him, our habits reflect the strength of our grit. We thrill to meet others who can help us in small or big ways. Our limited relationship capacity is redirected by grit's focus. This has practical implications for how we spend precious minutes with young people. *Choose joy.*

- *Don't settle for stabs of joy that randomly hit us while we surface skim through life.*
- *Don't imagine that waves of joy earned by exertions in shallow pursuits will satisfy.*
- *Gear up for disruptive, sustainable joy in a deep, portable relationship with Jesus.*

A few years ago, we experienced a widespread movement of God in my community that unnerved local youth ministers. I can still see the bewildered look of a seasoned veteran who pled with me: "What do I *do* now?" Years of youth ministry routines were being upended by the Holy Spirit's eye-opening activity in him and his teens.

Spending time to pursue intimacy with Christ will disrupt the pace of our days and weeks. Count on it. If we accept the challenge of meeting teens in their aimless surface skimming—where fragile joy is intertwined with hot and cold friendship experiences—we must be resolved to do everything we can to dive into Jesus' depth with them. Technological hacks can gain us shortcuts and microwaved meals may be tasty enough, but our speedy culture cannot hurry the permission needed to engage young people at soul-depth. Access to those mysteries require time-intensive, proven trustworthiness.

Had I veered through a suburban neighborhood heading home from the hospital on a Saturday night in 1984, I may have witnessed the grisly scene of a young man hanging himself from his driveway basketball hoop. I learned of the tragedy ten hours later. It was surreal to realize I would soon be bringing my newborn son into our home where Rod—now a suicide victim—had heard me urge him to trust Jesus only weeks earlier. The co-mingling of joy and sorrow was immediate and intense. Ajith Fernando wrote persuasively that this is the intersection ministers are called to inhabit.[262]

Rod had been living with his single mom. Her phone call early Sunday morning woke me with the news and her raw request for me to officiate at the funeral. The brief note Rod wrote revealed anguish we were unaware of: "I have no friends."

Suicide is an especially cruel accusation leveled against those who are left behind. The finality of death means no rebuttals will be heard. Those who mourned Rod thought of themselves as his friends. The message we wrestled with inside our shared loss was complex and revealing. We realized that what Rod gained from his friends and family was not enough for him. *We* were not enough to help him through his intolerable pain.

I believe that to be true. Ebonie's padded room encounter with Jesus aligns with the conviction we have about the pursuit of prevailing joy for families and young people: only God is enough. The stakes are high for the deep-diving arc of joy we want teens to take with us. Adults are failing young people. The evidence is clear. Throughout this book, we've made the case that only God is able to deliver joy durable enough to withstand adversity's assaults, be they incidental or overwhelming. We staked out the triangle of truths in which all of this can happen:

GOD IS LOVE.

JESUS IS LORD.

IT'S ALL GOOD.

Thankfully, faithful pilgrims have blazed the way for us. Years after Brother Lawrence washed his last dish in the presence of God, a nineteenth-century anonymous Russian wrote *The Way of a Pilgrim*. This book has acquainted many of us with a habitual practice connected to our heartbeat rhythms or breathing patterns so we can offer what's come to be known as the Jesus Prayer: While breathing in say "Lord Jesus Christ" and exhale the request, "have mercy on me."[263] The author revealed the grit of a *GUEST*—his perseverance to become Jesus-attentive was fruitful as he practiced for an hour at a time, then two hours, eventually training himself to sustain this praying for an entire day. As three weeks passed the anonymous witness testified to heartache giving way to joy. Love for Jesus, others, and creation became a powerful inner fire. This transformation seemed to bypass the efforts of thinking, though the pilgrim also reported he gained insights and understanding he couldn't explain. God was vividly present to him, and God's kingdom within him grew into certainty.[264] Please don't fail to notice that three weeks is not quite what we learned is the length of time it takes for habits as brain neuron highways to gain the white sheathing that unleashes their high speed, energy-saving performance.

Getting acquainted with the efforts of others wherever they may be found has fortified our own resolve in this journey. To know Jesus as our insistent, loving Pace Disruptor—and to welcome Him in that role—is to enjoy a familiar relationship with Him. We are essentially relational beings; what defines us as persons is the relationship we have with God.[265]

The Irish describe some locations as "thin places" between heaven and earth, where the veil is porous and God's presence seems more obvious.[266] But we share the conviction that we can experience "thin places" anywhere we are open to noticing Jesus,[267] who promised to be with us always.[268] A poor Caribbean island, a juvenile lock-up in rural Iowa, urban neighborhoods in Fort Wayne, Miami, Indianapolis, Columbus, Ferguson, a kitchen in 17th century Paris, a padded room near Washington D.C.— the presence of Jesus changes everything in every place. If we ignore Him in pursuit of sin, suddenly remember He is near, and yet willfully rebel, our hearts calcify. If we sense He's near, turn toward Him, and say "yes" to what had been "not yet," our hearts melt in the warmth of His love. To know Him is to love Him. Familiarity. Intimacy. A friendship like no other. Learning we are loved by Him excuses our vocabulary loss when others probe for explanations. Like Ebonie said, "Jesus. Just Jesus."

St. Teresa of Avila, a sixteenth-century Carmelite nun from Spain, was once dumped into some mud when she had a carriage mishap. Her response was directed at God, either with humor or petulance: "If this is the way you treat your friends, it's no wonder you have so few."[269] We choose to believe this was a good-natured exchange. Maybe that's because we have experienced Jesus as playful and enjoy the familiarity of being teased by Him. Childlike trust and intimacy expressed in laughter is, in our opinion, hard to beat.

There are lots of ways that this attribute could go sideways, and we don't want to defend all of the ridiculous possibilities that can be imagined when the Sovereign Lord of the Universe is also described as "playful." The word is evocative and hardly neutral. We're going to defend it. In fact, more youth ministers who understand playfulness may be just what the church needs—provided we locate the source of our laughter in the comfort of Jesus. C. S. Lewis appears to stand with us. His *Chronicles of Narnia* suggest there are times when a reassuring romp with the All Powerful One is just what we need. We wonder if St. Teresa would not urge skeptics to just start paying more attention to Jesus so they can actually enjoy His presence.

We experience less than durable joy because we haven't learned how to deep dive with Jesus. If you agree with us, we also hope grit-as-faith makes sense. When passion locks in, perseverance and innovation show up. Our gritty focus is life with Jesus. That's where joy's treasure is located. And that's why we think habits are the most honest form of revealing what's really important to us. In a sense, we're calling out anyone who says they want to experience joy with Jesus, whatever the cost: "OK. *Prove it.*"

Young people may overhear this as a hollow challenge among adults—an unlikely change—unless we've also met the authenticity test of joy with Jesus. Again, *prove it.*

Each of the four habits we suggest are carefully chosen pace disruptors to enhance a deep-diving, life-giving relationship with Jesus, characterized by prevailing joy. They can be done by young people, especially if gritty adults accompany them. *GUEST* is the habit picked to embolden us with a few friends who push, pull, shield, and challenge us. We join HERO (see chapter 5) profiled encouragers in concentrated time to swap fresh experiences with Jesus and pray together. *GUEST* allies connect at least weekly.

REST is the habit that helps self-aware Christ-followers live effectively in a world of relentless productivity and insistent restlessness. With revolutionary resistance[270] we set aside a day each week to disrupt the pace. Life will not easily spin out of control when we hit the reset button every seven days. God's original intent to provide such a rhythmic pause with Him fulfills a felt need. It makes gritty sense to leverage this time so we can better redeem every minute with Jesus. *REST* is a one-day per week routine.

INVEST is the habit that positions us for Jesus' intimate tutoring relationship. In the Bible's pages we get acquainted, and then fall in love, recovering Eden's garden status as naked and unashamed. He is safe, gentle, and humble. His way with us helps us experience trust's rest while He deals with raw nerve fibers bundling our identities. Everything about Jesus inspires humble grit. We dive into the depth of His heart to retrieve the choice pearl that's more valuable than anything we ever imagined when we set out on our quest. Joy with Jesus fuels our upward movement.[271] *INVEST* is a habit that is practiced five to seven days a week.

Finally, *TEST* is the habit that most puts us in the line of sight for a watching world. It pulls us into God's "witness reflection program." We glorify Him by testifying during life's tests that He—Jesus—is our intimate. He satisfies, empowers, and always coaxes us to explore more with Him. God's story co-mingles with our story in the retelling. Our joy prevails, authenticating us, and we know why: it's Jesus. Just Jesus. *TEST* makes most sense as a near daily practice when we circulate among others.

Joy is an always possible choice, available to the gritty who want to become more Jesus-*C*onnected, Jesus-*A*ttentive, Jesus-*R*esponsive, and Jesus-*A*uthentic (CARA) than they are. True to our playfulness in this writing, first letters for our four habits spell out *GRIT*. But as a nod to the mystery of grace that delivers joy, a Greek transliteration of the word for gladness is *CARA*. It's a giggly offering more than a profound truth to contemplate. But it's consistent with how we've learned to disrupt any norm in deep-diving with Jesus—and we're eager to enjoy your companionship as His *GUEST*.

ENDNOTES

[1] Matt Croasmun, "What's Worth Wanting," (opening plenary, Pedagogy of the Good Life conference hosted by the Yale Center for Faith and Culture, Yale Center for Faith and Culture, New Haven, CT, August 1, 2018).

[2] Angela Duckworth, *Grit* (New York: Scribner, 2016). A brief definition of this social science construct: When we embrace the clarity of a single passion and pursue it with uncommon perseverance, we discover the life-ordering power of grit.

[3] William A. Barry, SJ, *A Friendship Like No Other: Experiencing God's Amazing Embrace* (Chicago: Loyola Press, 2008).

[4] Psalm 42:7–8.

[5] Philip C. Watkins, Robert A. Emmons, Madeline R. Greaves, and Joshua Bell. 2017. "Joy Is a Distinct Positive Emotion: Assessment of Joy and Relationship to Gratitude and Well-Being." *The Journal of Positive Psychology* 13 (5): 522–39. doi:10.1080/17439760.2017.1414298.

[6] Dave Rahn, "Reckoning with Adolescent Influence: A Sociological Perspective," *Christian Education Journal,* 3 NS, no.2 (1999): 81–91.

[7] Donna Matthews, "Turn Off That Smartphone, Mom and Dad!" *Psychology Today,* November 23, 2017, https://www.psychologytoday.com/us/blog/going-beyond-intelligence/201711/turn-smartphone-mom-and-dad.

[8] Julia Naftulin, "Here's How Many Times We Touch Our Phones Every Day," *Business Insider,* July 13, 2016, https://www.businessinsider.com/dscout-research-people-touch-cell-phones-2617-times-a-day-2016-7.

[9] Susanna Schrobsdorff, "Teen Depression and Anxiety: Why the Kids Are Not Alright," *Time,* October 27, 2016, http://time.com/magazine/us/4547305/november-7th-2016-vol-188-no-19-u-s.

[10] Erika Christakis, "The Dangers of Distracted Parenting," *The Atlantic,* June 16, 2018. https://www.theatlantic.com/magazine/archive/2018/07/the-dangers-of-distracted-parenting/561752.

[11] Kenda Creasy Dean, *Almost Christian* (Oxford: Oxford University Press, 2010), 3–16.

[12] C. S. Lewis, *Surprised by Joy* (San Diego: Harcourt Brace Jovanovich, 1955), 218–222.

[13] Ibid., 238.

[14] Luke 19:10.

[15] John 8:1–11.

16 Note Paul's description of sin's pervasive, life-sucking spiral in Romans 1:18–32.

17 Luke 15:1–2, 11–32.

18 See https://en.wikisource.org/wiki/Westminster_Shorter_Catechism.

19 Dorothy Bass, *Receiving the Day* (San Francisco: Josey-Bass, 2000), 16.

20 1 John 4:8, 16.

21 The ESV records the word "love" in Matthew 10 times, Mark 3 times, and Luke 9 times; John's gospel uses the word 20 times. The "true/truth" usage differential is even more stark: Matthew 1 time, Mark 2 times, Luke 3 times, and John 41 times! John's three short epistles illustrate the lasting fruitfulness of this pairing, as he writes of "true/truth" 20 times and "love" 30 times.

22 Romans 11:36.

23 Let these verses awe you: Ephesians 1:9–11, 19–23; 2:19–22; 3:3–11; Philippians 2:5–11; Colossians 1:9–21; 2:1–10.

24 This is the force of Romans 8:28, as powerfully unpacked by N. T. Wright, *Into the Heart of Romans* (Grand Rapids, MI: Zondervan, 2023).

25 Philippians 4:4; James 1:2, ESV.

26 See the presentation of data from the U.S. Survey on Drug Use and Health as presented by Jonathan Haidt, *The Anxious Generation* (New York: Penguin Books, 2024), 27.

27 Augustine, *The Confessions of St. Augustine* (Garden City, NY: Doubleday Image Book, 1960), trans., John K. Ryan, 43.

28 Skye Jethani, *With: Reimagining the Way You Relate to God* (Nashville: Thomas Nelson, 2011).

29 Daniel Kahneman, *Thinking, Fast and Slow* (New York: Farrar, Straus and Giroux, 2011), 29.

30 This is a point reinforced repeatedly by Marcus Warner and Jim Wilder, *Rare Leadership* (Chicago: Moody Publishers, 2016).

31 Discussed at length by Warner and Wilder. A primary source is one of the published works by UCLA researcher Allan Schore, e.g., *Affect Regulation and the Origin of the Self: The Neurobiology of Emotional Development* (Hove, UK: Psychology Press, 2012).

32 Warner and Wilder, *Rare Leadership,* 71.

33 Ibid., 64–65.

34 John 15:15.

35 John 15:11.

36 Barry, *A Friendship Like No Other.*

37 In the 1981 movie, *Chariots of Fire,* the character playing missionary and British Olympian, Eric Liddell, explained the joy of his athletic endeavors to his sister with this iconic line: "When I run, I feel His pleasure."

38 Galatians 5:22.

39 This is derived from the notion of adolescents' "personal fables," discussed by David Elkind, *All Grown Up and No Place to Go* (Reading, MA: Addison-Wesley, 1984), 34–36.

40 1 Thessalonians 5:16.

41 Marcus Warner and Stefanie Hinman, *Building Bounce* (Carmel, IN: Deeper Walk International, 2020), 17–23.

42 James 1:2.

43 John 16:33.

44 Remember the character Neo in *The Matrix* or how 'The Force' in *Star Wars* works? They are transcendent!

45 We first heard this phrase from Rick Lawrence.

46 For further exploration and resources, check out https://yfc.net/about/3story/.

47 Twenty One Pilots, "Addict with a Pen," by Tyler Joseph, Chris Salih, and Nick Thomas, recorded ca. 2008–2009, track 4 on *Twenty One Pilots,* 2009, compact disc.

48 A phrase used by Miroslav Volf, "Becoming Practical Theologians of Joy," (plenary address, Association of Youth Ministry Educators, St. Louis, MO, October 27, 2018).

49 "Landmark Report: U.S. Teens Use an Average of Nine Hours of Media Per Day, Tweens Use Six Hours," Common Sense Media, November 3. 2015, https://www.commonsensemedia.org/press-releases/landmark-report-us-teens-use-an-average-of-nine-hours-of-media-per-day-tweens-use-six-hours.

50 Mark Buchanan, *The Rest of God* (Nashville: Thomas Nelson, 2006), 35.

51 Isaiah 55:1–2.

52 Christian Smith with Melinda Lundquist Denton, *Soul Searching* (New York: Oxford University Press, 2005), 162–170.

53 Ephesians 3:19.

54 John 15:5.

55 Philippians 4:4; 1 Thessalonians 5:16.

56 Matthew 7:15–20.

57 Galatians 5:22–23.

58 John 15:1–17.

[59] Consider how Paul's teaching in Galatians 2:11–5:6 about the role and limitations of the law; it cannot actually free us for Spirit-led (joyful) living and undergirds the discussion to follow.

[60] "Scientists Study Nomophobia—Fear of Being without a Mobile Phone," *Scientific American,* October 27, 2015. https://www.scientificamerican.com/article/scientists-study-nomophobia-mdash-fear-of-being-without-a-mobile-phone/.

[61] Haidt, *The Anxious Generation,* 65.

[62] While their research found that more than half of Gen Z (57%) use screen media more than four hours a day, some (26%) spend eight hours or more daily looking at digital screens, Barna Group, *Gen Z: The Culture, Beliefs and Motivations Shaping the Next Generation* (Ventura, CA: Barna Group, 2018), 14–15.

[63] Tim Elmore, "Nomophopbia: A Rising Trend in Students," *Psychology Today*, September 18, 2014, https://www.psychologytoday.com/us/blog/artificial-maturity/201409/nomophobia-a-rising-trend-in-students.

[64] Allison Hydzik, "Using lots of social media sites raises depression risk," University of Pittsburg Brain Institute, revised August 28, 2024, http://www.braininstitute.pitt.edu/using-lots-social-media-sites-raises-depression-risk.

[65] Jenny Anderson, "Even teens are worried they spend too much time on their phones," *Quartz*, August 13, 2018, https://qz.com/1367506/pew-research-teens-worried-they-spend-too-much-time-on-phones/.

[66] Watkins, et. al., "Joy is a Distinct Positive Emotion," 533.

[67] Ibid., 525–530.

[68] Ibid., 531–533.

[69] Buchanan, *The Rest of God,* 200.

[70] Matthew 7:21–23.

[71] John 14:15, 21, 24; 15:10.

[72] Graham Kendrick, "Knowing You Jesus," track 2 on *Graham Kendrick Ultimate Collection,* Integrity Music, 2015, compact disc.

[73] Proverbs 4:23.

[74] John 21:20–22.

[75] "Home." The Great Opportunity. Accessed October 4, 2024. https://www.greatopportunity.org/.

[76] This phrase is akin to what Jim Denison often writes, as any loyal reader of his daily blog might know (https://www.denisonforum.org/).

[77] 1 Thessalonians 5:16.

78 Hebrews 12:1–2.

79 Genesis 2:18.

80 Smith and Denton, *Soul Searching.*

81 E.g., Christian Smith, with Patricia Snell, *Souls in Transition: The Religious and Spiritual Lives of Emerging Adults* (New York: Oxford University Press, 2009); Kenda Creasy Dean, *Almost Christian: What the Faith of our Teenagers Is Telling the American Church* (New York: Oxford University Press, 2010); Lisa D. Pearce and Melissa Lundquist Denton, *A Faith of Their Own: Stability and Change in the Religiosity of America's Adolescents* (New York: Oxford University Press, 2011); Christian Smith and Amy Adamczyk, *Handing Down the Faith: How Parents Pass Their Religion on to the Next Generation* (New York: Oxford University Press, 2021).

82 Dean, *Almost Christian,* 3–4.

83 Richly articulated in Carl Trueman, *Strange New World: How Thinkers and Activists Redefined Identity and Sparked the Sexual Revolution* (Wheaton, IL: Crossway, 2022).

84 The phrase "expressive individualism" was used by Robert N. Bellah, Richard Madsen, William M. Sullivan, Ann Swidler, and Steven M. Tipton, *Habits of the Heart: Individualism and Commitment in American Life* (Berkely: University of California Press, 1985), 333–34.

85 In this philosophical work, *authenticity* is offered as an essential description of our culture. Charles Taylor, *A Secular Age* (Cambridge, MA: Belknap, 2007), 475.

86 Trueman, *Strange New World,* 23.

87 Christiam Smith and Adam Adamczyk, *Handing Down the Faith: How Parents Pass Their Religion on to the Next Generation* (New York: Oxford University Press, 2021), Conclusion, location 4845–4864, Kindle.

88 See especially Chapters 2 and 3 in Chap Clark, *Hurt 2.0: Inside the World of Today's Teenagers* (Grand Rapids, MI: Baker Academic, 2011), 23–56.

89 Daniel Kahneman, Olivier Sibony, and Cass R. Sunstein, *Noise: A Flaw in Human Judgment* (New York: Little, Brown Spark/Hachette Book Group, 2021).

90 Robin Dunbar, *Friends: Understanding the Power of Our Most Important Relationships* (London: Little, Brown/Hachette Book Group, 2021).

91 We pounced on this insight as a result of contemplating the intersection of two books: Jim Wilder, *Renovated: God, Dallas Willard, and the Church that Transforms* (Colorado Springs, CO: Shepherd's House/NavPress, 2020) and James Clear, *Atomic Habits* (New York: Avery Books/Random House, 2018).

[92] Richelle White, "Mentors of Joy," (plenary address during the closing session of Association of Youth Ministry Educators, St. Louis, MO, October 29, 2018).

[93] A succinct summary of Albert Bandura's social learning research about modeling which we employ here is found in Lawrence O. Richards, *Christian Education* (Grand Rapids: Zondervan, 1975), 84–85.

[94] Dave Rahn, "Unlocking the Keys to Indigenous Urban Leadership," *Journal of Youth Ministry* 11, no.2 (Spring 2013).

[95] Smith and Adamczyk, *Handing Down the Faith,* 4882–4889, Kindle.

[96] Rahn, "Unlocking the Keys to Indigenous Urban Leadership," 29–40.

[97] E.g., Smith and Adamczyk, *Handing Down the Faith,* 4891, Kindle; Kelly Dean Schwartz, "Transformations in Parent and Friend Faith Support Predicting Adolescents' Religious Faith," *International Journal for the Psychology of Religion*, 16, no.4 (2006), 311–326; Dave Rahn, "Reckoning with Adolescent Influence: A Sociological Perspective" *Christian Education Journal* 3NS, no.2 (Fall 1999), 81–91; Dave Rahn and Terry Linhart, *Evangelism Remixed: Empowering Students for Courageous and Contagious Faith* (Grand Rapids: Youth Specialties/Zondervan, 2009); Amanda Hontz Drury, *Saying is Believing: The Necessity of Testimony in Adolescent Spiritual Development* (Downers Grove, IL: IVP Academic, 2015).

[98] Josh Packard, *The State of Religion & Young People 2020: Relational Authority* (Winona, MN: Springtide Research Institute, 2020).

[99] Ibid.

[100] Clark, *Hurt 2.0.*

[101] Arthur Holmes, *All Truth is God's Truth* (Grand Rapids, MI: Eerdmans, 1977).

[102] Saving faith is solely a work of God in those who believe in Christ. Scripture also lists faith as a gift of the Holy Spirit that can be given in varying degrees to different believers. This is the aspect of faith that shares similarities with grit.

[103] Angela Duckworth, *Grit* (New York, NY: Scribner, 2016).

[104] Ibid., 247–250.

[105] Ibid., 3.

[106] Ibid., 42.

[107] Ibid., 8.

[108] Malcom Gladwell, *Outliers: The Story of Success* (New York: Little, Brown and Company, 2008), 39.

[109] E.g., Matthew 16:24; Mark 8:34; Luke 9:23; John 12:23–26; Galatians 2:20; Philippians 3:7–11; Colossians 2:6–15.

110 Mark 3:14.

111 Matthew 28:19–20.

112 Acts 4:13.

113 John 5:6, ESV.

114 For a quick introduction that illuminates clearly why grit has a correlational connection with a growth mindset see Carol Dweck, *Mindset* (New York: Ballantine Books, Random House, 2008), 6–12.

115 Exodus 20:8.

116 Lewis, *Surprised by Joy,* 238.

117 See Matthew 11:28–30.

118 While we heartily recommend the entire book to unpack these distinctions, a brief summary can be found in Jethani, *With*, 100–101.

119 Luke 13:10–17.

120 Luke 13:18–21.

121 Bracelets with these initials were intended to give wearers pause to consider "What Would Jesus Do?"

122 2 Timothy 3:5.

123 Hosea 6:1–7.

124 1 Samuel 13:14; Acts 13:22.

125 Psalm 51:16–19.

126 Psalm 40:6–8.

127 1 Samuel 24.

128 1 Samuel 21:6.

129 Mark 2:25–28.

130 Psalm 51:4.

131 See John 13:23; 19:26; 20:2; 21:7, 20.

132 John 3:16.

133 1 John 4:8, 16.

134 John 20:21.

135 Kahneman, *Thinking, Fast and Slow,* 23.

136 Dunbar, *The Science of Love,* 136–137.

137 Mark 3:14.

138 Mark 5:37; 9:2; 14:33.

139 Buchanan, *The Rest of God,* 138.

140 Luke 14:12–14, 26.

[141] Duckworth, *Grit,* 55.

[142] Duckworth, *Grit,* 56.

[143] Merton Strommen, Karen E. Jones, and Dave Rahn, *Youth Ministry that Transforms* (Grand Rapids, MI: Zondervan, 2001), 47.

[144] 1 Corinthians 2:6–16.

[145] Matthew 11:28–30.

[146] Francisco Goya, "Saturn Devouring His Son," ca. 1820–1823, mixed media mural transferred to canvas, 143.5 cm x 81.4 cm (56.5 in x 32 in), Museo del Padro, Madrid, Spain, https://en.wikipedia.org/wiki/Saturn_Devouring_His_Son.

[147] Barry, *A Friendship Like No Other,* 100.

[148] Mihaly Csikszentmihalyi, *Flow: The Psychology of Optimal Experience* (New York: Harper Collins, 1990).

[149] Ezekiel 20:10–12.

[150] Psalm 46:10.

[151] Philippians 3:8.

[152] We recommend a slow, prayerful, open-hearted read through two of Paul's short epistles, Galatians and Ephesians, to let this beautiful truth sink in.

[153] Matthew 11:28–30, The Message.

[154] Hebrews 12:2.

[155] Exodus 20:8.

[156] A personal note: I have not connected with Frank for over a year, *but at the very moment* I was rewriting this section about him, he sent me an out-of-the-blue text of encouragement. Script followers step aside. I'm becoming an improv artist addicted to Jesus' joyful rigging of *ALL THINGS!*—DR

[157] Luke 5:1–11.

[158] Andrew Hill, *Be Quick—But Don't Hurry: Finding Success in the Teachings of a Lifetime* (New York: Simon & Schuster, 2001).

[159] Matthew 8:23–27; Mark 4:35–41; Luke 8:22–25.

[160] Colossians 1:17.

[161] The song we're referencing here is "This Is Me" for the movie *The Greatest Showman.* Keala Settle, vocalist, "This Is Me," by Justin Paul and Benj Pasek, recorded 2017, track 7 on *The Greatest Showman: Original Motion Picture Soundtrack,* Atlantic Records, compact disc.

[162] Isaiah 56:1–8.

[163] Jeremiah 17:21–27.

[164] Ezekiel 20:10–26.

165 Colossians 3:1–4.

166 See the substantial research to support this conclusion in Leidy Klotz, *Subtract* (New York: Flatiron Books, 2021).

167 John 15:2.

168 Matthew 5:17.

169 Romans 12:2.

170 1 Corinthians 2:16.

171 See 1 Corinthians 3:5–9.

172 Warner and Wilder, *Rare Leadership,* 29.

173 Words by Richard of Chichester (att., c. 1197–1253), published as "Hymn 654" in *The Hymnal 1982* (New York, NY: Church Publishing Incorporated, 1985).

174 Sheldon Vanauken, *A Severe Mercy* (New York: Harper & Row, 1977), 37.

175 Revelation 2:1–7.

176 Warner and Wilder, *Rare Leadership,* 117.

177 Ibid., 116.

178 Galatians 2:20–21; 3:3.

179 Revelation 3:20.

180 See Jesus' powerful teaching and example-setting with Mary and Martha in Luke 10:38–42.

181 Matthew 18:15–20.

182 Frank Newport, "2017 Update on Americans and Religion," Gallup, December 22, 2017, https://news.gallup.com/poll/224642/2017-update-americans-religion.aspx.

183 "Where Americans Find Meaning in Life," Pew Research Center, November 20, 2018, http://www.pewforum.org/2018/11/20/where-americans-find-meaning-in-life.

184 Em Griffin, *The Mindchangers* (Wheaton, IL: Tyndale, 1976), 200.

185 Rahn, "Reckoning with Adolescent Influence," 84–85.

186 Smith and Adamczyk, *Handing Down the Faith*, chapter 3, location 1977–1982, Kindle.

187 Revelation 2:17.

188 Ephesians 4:16.

189 Stephen R. Covey, *First Things First* (New York, NY: Simon & Schuster, 1994), 88–90.

190 Buchanan, *The Rest of God,* 45.

[191] Ruth Haley Barton, *Sacred Rhythms: Arranging Our Lives for Spiritual Transformation* (Downers Grove, IL: IVP Books, 2006), 139.

[192] This idea was developed as a result of sweetly generous insights about Sabbath practice offered by Kara Root.

[193] Isaiah 40:28.

[194] Buchanan, *The Rest of God,* 138.

[195] Walter Brueggemann, *Sabbath as Resistance: Saying No to the Culture of Now* (Louisville, KY: Westminster John Knox Press, 2014), 45.

[196] E.g., Matthew 11:25, 18:3, 19:14.

[197] Rick Lawrence, *Jesus-Centered Daily* (Group Publishing, June 19, 2020).

[198] The citation here and in notes to follow draw from a classic work originally published in 1692; to assist the reader interested in finding this content they have been derived from a modern edition. Brother Lawrence, *The Practice of the Presence of God* (New Kensington, PA: Whitaker House, 1982), First Letter, 11.

[199] See Paul's testimony in Philippians 3:1–16 for an example of this intent.

[200] Brother Lawrence, *The Practice of the Presence of God,* Fourth Conversation, 24.

[201] Ibid., First Letter, 29–31.

[202] Matthew 11:28–30.

[203] Brother Lawrence, *The Practice of the Presence of God,* Second Letter, 32–33.

[204] Ibid., Second Conversation, 13–15.

[205] Ibid., Fourth Conversation, 22–24.

[206] Ibid., First Conversation, 11.

[207] Ibid., First Letter, 29.

[208] 1 Thessalonians 5:16–18.

[209] Warner and Wilder, *Rare Leadership,* 24.

[210] This insightful observation came from my friend Drew while we devoured breakfast at an Amish restaurant.

[211] David Kinnaman and Mark Matlock, *Faith for Exiles* (Grand Rapids, MI: Baker Books, 2019), 50.

[212] Shakespeare, *The Tragedy of Hamlet, Prince of Denmark,* 3.1.1749.

[213] Philippians 3:8–9.

[214] Philippians 3:12–14.

[215] Philippians 3:15–16.

[216] Philippians 3:17.

217 Matthew 11:28–30.

218 John 10:4–5, 14–16.

219 Matthew 13:10–17.

220 Matthew 7:24–27.

221 See Jeremiah 42:19–22 for a representative description of the unfaithful.

222 Revelation 2:7, 11, 17, 29; 3:6, 13, 22.

223 Psalm 95:7–8.

224 See Hebrews 3:7–4:7 for a summary of how hardheartedness has consistently disqualified us from restfulness with God.

225 Hebrews 4:12–16.

226 Jeffery Fulks, Angel Mann, Randy Petersen, and John Plake, *State of the Bible 2024* (Philadelphia, PA: American Bible Society, 2024), 3, https://www.americanbible.org/wp-content/uploads/2024/09/SOTB-2024-09_Final-v2.pdf.

227 Greg L. Hawkins and Cally Parkinson, *Move* (Grand Rapids, MI: Zondervan, 2011), 259–263.

228 Ibid., 69–119.

229 Matthew 6:24–34; Romans 12:1–2; Ephesians 4:17–23; Philippians 4:6–8; Colossians 3:1–4; 2 Timothy 4:3–5.

230 Duckworth, *Grit,* 137–138.

231 See 1 Samuel 13:14 and Acts 13:22.

232 Stefon Harris, "There Are No Mistakes in the Bandstand," TED on YouTube, December 9, 2011, video, 13:11, https://www.youtube.com/watch?v=7shXEFuxHAA.

233 Rick Lawrence, *Jesus-Centered Daily*, March 17 entry.

234 Vivek H. Murthy, "Surgeon General: Why I'm Calling for a Warning Label on Social Media Platforms," *New York Times,* June 17, 2024, https://www.nytimes.com/2024/06/17/opinion/social-media-health-warning.html#.

235 Jason Ingram, Lauren Daigle, Paul Mabury, "Love Like This," track 7 on *Look Up Child,* 2018, Centricity Music, compact disc; Hank Bentley, Jason Ingram, Lauren Daigle, Mia Fieldes, Paul Mabury, "First," track 1 on *How Can It Be,* 2015, Centricity Music, compact disc; Lauren Daigle, Michael Farren, Paul Mabury, "Trust In You," track 3 on *How Can It Be,* 2015, Centricity Music, compact disc; Jason Ingram, Lauren Daigle, Paul Mabury, "You Say," track 5 on *Look Up Child,* 2018, Centricity Music, compact disc; Jason Ingram, Lauren Daigle, Paul Mabury, "Look Up Child," track 8 on *Look Up Child, Deluxe Edition,* 2022, Centricity Music, compact disc.

236 John 10:10.

[237] E.g., 2 Corinthians 4:1–16, Ephesians 2:4–10, and Philippians 2:5–13.

[238] Charles Haddon Spurgeon, "Deep Calleth Unto Deep," The Spurgeon Center. Sermon originally delivered on April 11, 1869, access date November 26, 2018, https://www.spurgeon.org/resource-library/sermons/deep-calleth-unto-deep#flipbook/.

[239] Ibid.

[240] Louis shared his love for scuba diving with Dave on November 25, 2019.

[241] From Dave's conversation with Elizabeth on November 6, 2019, in Kansas City, where she has a thriving therapy practice.

[242] Colossians 2:6–7.

[243] Colossians 2:2.

[244] Colossians 1:27.

[245] Colossians 3:3.

[246] From a reunion conversation Dave had with Sabrina Mason on November 29, 2019.

[247] Dave served as one of the founding board members for *Presence Point*, a ministry that helps leaders assume the responsibility of shepherds to be present, provide and protect those under their care. "Live into your calling" is one of their signature statements. See www.presencepoint.com.

[248] Charles Duhigg, *The Power of Habit* (New York, NY: Random House, 2014), 59.

[249] Warner and Wilder, *Rare Leadership*, 156.

[250] Brother Lawrence, *The Practice of the Presence of God*, Third Conversation, 21.

[251] Duhigg, *The Power of Habit*, 100.

[252] The Book of Job and Jesus' words in Luke 22:31–32 reveal this.

[253] John 15:2.

[254] James 1:2–4.

[255] 1 Corinthians 15:5–8.

[256] Acts 1:8.

[257] 1 Peter 3:15–16.

[258] Luke 6:45.

[259] Amanda Drury, *Saying is Believing*, 42.

[260] Ibid., 53.

[261] Griffin, *The Mindchangers*, 181.

[262] Ajith Fernando, *The Call to Joy and Pain* (Wheaton, IL: Crossway Books, 2007).

263 *The Way of a Pilgrim,* trans. Nina Toumanova (Garden City, NY: Dover Publications, 2008), 31; 62.

264 Ibid., 31–32.

265 Barry, *A Friendship Like No Other,* 14.

266 Ibid., 163.

267 Ibid., 176.

268 Matthew 28:20.

269 Barry, *A Friendship Like No Other,* 127. Barry quoted St. Teresa in the opening of his Chapter 10.

270 Brueggemann, *Sabbath as Resistance.*

271 Matthew 13:45–46.